Trailerama

Trailerama

Phil Noyes

An Invitation...

to Gracious Living

GIBBS SMITH
TO ENRICH AND INSPIRE HUMANKIND

First Edition
16 15 14 13 12   5 4 3 2 1

Text © 2012 Phil Noyes

Published by
Gibbs Smith
P.O. Box 667
Layton, Utah 84041

1.800.835.4993 orders
www.gibbs-smith.com

Designed by Kurt Wahlner
Printed and bound in China

Gibbs Smith books are printed on either recycled, 100% post-consumer waste, FSC-certified papers or on paper produced from sustainable PEFC-certified forest/controlled wood source. Learn more at www.pefc.org.

Library of Congress Control Number: 2012937604

ISBN: 978-1-4236-2142-3

All contemporary photography by Marty Snortum. All other images courtesy of the author, except as noted below:

Pages 1, 25, 27 (bottom left & right), 30 (top center), 76–77 (background), 86 (bottom left), 121 (background), 132 (top left), 135 (top right), 136, 137 (bottom right), 139 (top left, bottom right), 140–41 (various images), 143, 144 (top second from left), 145 (top left), 146 (bottom left), 147 (top, bottom left), 151, 155, 156 (background), 157 (background), 161 (background), 166, 167 (bottom left), 168 (bottom), 169 (top, bottom right), 170–71 (all color images), back cover: Charles Phoenix Collection.

Pages 2, 30 (center, bottom center), 71 (bottom right), 72, 92–93, 94 (bottom right), 102 (bottom right), 133 (top right), endsheets: Los Angeles Public Library, Los Angeles Herald Examiner Photograph Collection.

Pages 5, 116–17: Images provided by Steven Butcher. Permission granted by Webster Golinkin. Painted in 1935 by Joseph Webster Golinkin.

Pages 6-7: Shady Dell.

Pages 8, 19 (left), 27 (top left), 28 (bottom right), 30 (top right), 33 (top left, bottom right), 41 (bottom right), 44 (bottom left), 45 (top & bottom left, bottom right), 46 (bottom right), 50–51, 53 (right), 58 (top & bottom left), 61, 63 (top & bottom left), 64 (bottom right), 65 (top left), 66 (right), 67, 70 (bottom left), 75 (top), 78 (bottom right), 87 (top left), 100 (left), 145 (bottom), 173 (bottom right), 175 (top right): Vince Martinico.

Page 9 (top): Margaret Martan.

Pages 9 (bottom), 19 (top & bottom right), 20 (top right), 23 (bottom right), 24 (bottom left), 27 (top right), 28 (top left), 29 (bottom right), 33 (top right), 37 (bottom left), 40 (left), 41 (top & bottom left), 43 (top left & right, bottom), 44 (bottom center), 46 (top right), 66 (bottom left), 70 (top right), 89 (bottom right), 94 (top, center far left), 100 (top right), 101 (top left & center), 111 (bottom four images), 113 (top left, bottom left), 127 (top left & right, bottom left), 129 (bottom left), 130 (bottom right), 132 (right, bottom

left), 133 (bottom right), 134 (top left), 135 (bottom left), 140–41 (various images), 154 (bottom left), 161 (bottom left), 167 (top right), 172 (center right): John Agnew.

Pages 10–15, 18 (bottom right): Bergman Collection.

Pages 16–17, 28 (bottom left), 29 (left), 31, 32 (right), 34, 115 (bottom left), 120 (center left), 129 (top right), 140–41 (various images), 152 (bottom left), 154 (top): David Woodworth.

Pages 18 (top right), 30 (top left), 35 (bottom right), 36 (bottom left), 37 (top left), 73 (top right), 101 (bottom right), 128 (top right), 134 (top right), 140–41 (various images), 144 (bottom left), 154 (bottom right), endsheets: Steven Butcher.

Pages 20 (bottom right), 23 (top right), 37 (right), 44 (top & bottom right), 60 (bottom row), 66 (left center), 135 (center left), 161 (top center), 169 (bottom left): David Izenman.

Pages 24 (top left), 60 (top left), 68, 70 (bottom right), 133 (bottom left), 181 (top right): Chris Hart.

Pages 24 (top right), 175 (bottom), 181 (center right), 182, 184–91: Wallace Collection.

Pages 26, 29 (top right), 35 (bottom left, top right), 69, 75 (bottom), 102 (bottom left): USC Libraries, Special Collections Department.

Page 30 (bottom left): Library of Congress, Prints & Photographs Division. Photograph by Harris & Ewing, LC-DIG-hec-22816.

Pages 32 (left), 108, 133 (top left): Courtesy of *Popular Mechanics*. Originally published in the August 1939 issue.

Page 36 (top left): Los Angeles Public Library, Los Angeles Herald Examiner Photograph Collection. Photograph by Fred Dapprich.

Pages 40 (right), 47, 89 (top), 107, 122–23, 138 (bottom), 140–41 (various images), endsheets: Watson Family Archive.

Pages 42 (right), 46 (bottom left), 121 (center), 173 (bottom center): Tim Heinz.

Page 49: Richard Miller.

Page 52: Garrett Price/*New Yorker* magazine © Condé Nast Publications. Originally published in the September 15, 1951 issue.

Page 53 (left): Roger Duvoisin/*New Yorker*

magazine © Condé Nast Publications. Originally published in the February 8, 1941 issue.

Page 54: Illustration © SEPS. Licensed by Curtis Licensing. All rights reserved.

Pages 55 (left), 83: Automobile Club of Southern California Archives.

Pages 57 (right), 65 (right), 75 (center), 77 (top & bottom left), 84 (top left, bottom left), 86 (top center & right), 89 (bottom left), 111 (top left & right), 178–79: Glenn Jensen.

Pages 74, 78 (bottom left): Courtesy of *Popular Mechanics*. Originally published in the December 1936 issue.

Pages 76, 88, 94 (bottom left), 101 (top right), 102 (center left), 118–19, 140–41 (various images), 161 (top right): Milton Newman.

Page 81: Los Angeles Public Library, Los Angeles Herald Examiner Photograph Collection. Photograph by Art Streib.

Pages 96–97: Larry Shank.

Pages 101 (center right), 105 (top), 114 (bottom center), 115 (top), 125, 126 (top left), 128 (bottom right), 144 (top second from right): Steve Walker.

Page 102 (top left): Library of Congress, Prints & Photographs Division. Photograph by Harris & Ewing, LC-DIG-hec-23246.

Page 102 (top right): Library of Congress, Prints & Photographs Division. Photograph by Harris & Ewing, LC-DIG-hec-23247.

Page 103 (top left): Caroline Kozo Cole.

Page 103 (right): Courtesy of *Popular Mechanics*. Originally published in the May 1936 issue.

Page 106: Reproduced by permission of The Huntington Library, San Marino, California.

Page 120 (top left & right): Terry Bone.

Page 131: Permission granted by Jack Howe. Cartoons by Bill O'Malley.

Pages 140–41 (various images), 163: Leo Keoshian.

Page 144 (bottom right): Library of Congress, Prints & Photographs Division, FSA-OWI Collection, LC-USF33-T0-000809.

Page 165 (top right): Los Angeles Public Library, Ansel Adams Collection.

Page 167 (top left): Cathy McNassor.

ACKNOWLEDGMENTS

The author would like to thank Charles Phoenix, for not only the use of his incredible collection but also his support throughout this experience; David Izenman, for being the best BFF a guy could ever want; John Agnew, Steven Butcher and Ed Lum from Funky Junk Farms, for being the pioneers that you are and for doing so much to keep our crazy little subculture alive; Terry and Forest Bone, and all the members of the Tin Can Tourists—may the club last another hundred years; Vince Martinico and Milton Newman, for being so generous in so many ways; Kurt Wahlner, for being the best darn designer around and putting up with me, and his wife, Joanne, for all the great meals; Marty Snortum, for driving ten thousand miles to take the best pictures a guy could ask for, and the Bergmans and Henry Wallace, for letting Marty into your homes to take those snaps; my brothers Nick and Jim, for always having the time to listen and all the love and support; and most importantly, my wife Lisa . . . you are my partner in crime and the most beautiful trailerite in all the land!

I can't thank everybody who has contributed to this book, but here are just a few that need a special thank you: Tim Heinz, Glenn Jensen, David Woodworth, Larry Shank, Dan Watson, Antoinette Watson, Caroline Kozo Cole, Dace Taube, Steve Walker, Margaret Martan, Web Golinkin, Harry Pallenberg, Chris Hart, Craig Dorsey, Scott Burud, Justin and Jen at the Shady Dell, Nevena Christi, Jack Howe, Morgan Yates, Leo and Marlys Keoshian, Cathy McNassor, Al Hesselbart, Michael Andrews, Reece Vogel, Chuck and Toni Miltinberger, Christie and Richard, Marge and Jeff, and Joey and Tia.

Dedicated to my parents.
Thanks for putting up with my shenanigans all these years.

INTRODUCTION

Let me start by saying this book is not a history lesson, nor am I a historian. I am just a guy who loves vintage trailers and all the wonderful ephemera that has come out of this industry over the last hundred years.

I am the guy at the flea market who is sitting in the dirt with a box full of a thousand musty snapshots looking for just one that may feature a travel trailer on some long-forgotten adventure. Maybe a faded black-and-white Polaroid with the snaggletooth edges of a happy family midway through a cross-country adventure, with their home-on-wheels swaying along behind them; or a Kodachrome slide of little Bobby and Jenny posing in front of the family's new Airstream parked in their 1950s suburban driveway. I also spend an inordinate amount of time and money on eBay searching for just one more bit of trailer-related paperwork, and have been known to go a little crazy during a bidding war for something so obscure that most people wouldn't give it a second look.

But I am not alone! Oh, no. . . . There is a small army of crazy, like-minded trailerites out there sitting in the dirt and scouring the Internet for vintage goodies, and our ranks are growing! We get together at rallies and swap stories and buy and sell and trade those odd finds that mean so much to us. We drag our vintage trailers with us, and of course all our camping gear is vintage and usually specific to our trailers. God forbid your 1947 Westcraft would have a lounge chair from the sixties under the awning (made from original painted duck canvas, of course), and the horror if somebody shows up who has thrown out all the original appliances and traded them for something modern!

We like our stuff with a story and a soul . . . a little rust is OK and some patina is always a plus. But what is it that feeds our passion? Why are we so in love with these old trailers? For me, they're akin to a time capsule. Each trailer and every scrap of paper, each little toy, and especially the snapshots, are windows into our collective pasts. I can spend hours looking at old brochures and ads, just marveling at the hand-drawn images that we so rarely see now, or the lovely models in their fabulous bathing attire toweling off after a shower in their 1930s Land Yacht.

This book pays homage to all things vintage trailer, and I hope that all you nontrailerites will find these images as lovely and engaging as I do. I know I am preaching to the choir for those of you who are already in our little "trailer tribe," but I think you will find some surprises lurking in these pages. There are so many tales to be told about this part of our American pop culture, and I have tried to give a wide overview through all the wonderful images that so many of my friends have graciously loaned for this book. So instead of spending hours perched over dusty tables at swap meets or scouring the Internet, we can all curl up and marvel at the glorious travel trailer. Welcome to *Trailerama*!

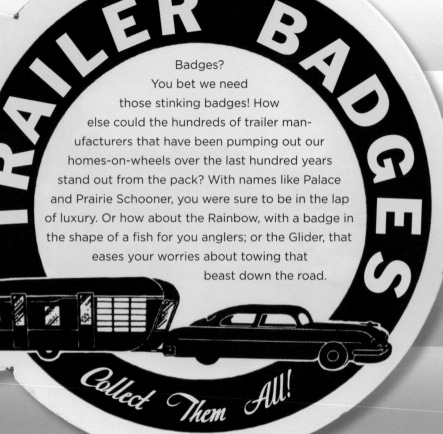

TRAILER BADGES

Badges?
You bet we need
those stinking badges! How
else could the hundreds of trailer manufacturers that have been pumping out our
homes-on-wheels over the last hundred years
stand out from the pack? With names like Palace
and Prairie Schooner, you were sure to be in the lap
of luxury. Or how about the Rainbow, with a badge in
the shape of a fish for you anglers; or the Glider, that
eases your worries about towing that
beast down the road.

Collect Them All!

Shasta®
TRAILERS
MFG BY
SHASTA TRAILERS, INC. OF INDIANA
812 LOGAN ST. GOSHEN INDIANA

Prairie Schooner
ELKHART IND. ELKTON MD.

RAINBOW
EDWARDS MFG. CO.

THE
DETROITER
COACH

SPARTAN
Imperial
Mansion
MFD. BY
SPARTAN AIRCRAFT CO.
TULSA, OKLAHOMA

BOLES AERO

STEWART
COACH

Continental
TRAILER COMPANY
CHICAGO

APACHE
VESELY MFG. LAPEER, MICHIGAN

AIRSTREAM

ZEPHYR
TRAILER
CHICAGO, ILLINOIS

TROTWOOD

VAGABOND

REDMAN TRAILER CO.
NEW MOON
ALMA, MICHIGAN

KOZY
Coach
KALAMAZOO, MICH.

SANTA FE
TRAILERS
SUN VALLEY, CALIF.

TRAVELO

THE COVERED WAGON
MOUNT CLEMENS, MICH.
REG. U.S. PAT. OFF.

SILVER ARROW
KENOSHA   CUSTOM   WIS.

McDONALD
DETROIT - SARASOTA
WORLD'S LARGEST

Travelo
SAGINAW

Serro Scotty
SPORTSMAN

ALMA

4009
PONTIAC
Chief
DRAYTON PLAINS
MICHIGAN

ROCKET 27
ALL STATES TRAILER CO.
JACKSONVILLE, ARK.

Streamlite 6

CURTISS

AEROCAR

SERIAL NO.   MODEL NO.

MADE IN
IN THE UNITED STATES   U.S.A.
PATENT NO 1880844   IN CANADA
PATENT DES 85815   PATENTED 1929 REISSUED 1933
PATENT DES 85816   IN GREAT BRITAIN
                             PATENT NO 313145 JUNE 8 1928

CURTISS AEROCAR COMPANY INC   CORAL GABLES FLORIDA

INDIAN TRAILER CORPORATION
CHICAGO

SCHULT

Ventoura

ELWOOD, INDIANA

Casa Mañana

HOUSE OF TOMORROW

by HENSLEE of Arlington, Texas

SER. NO. 55-1571

Brentwood

CHICAGO. ILL.

"M"

"M" SYSTEM
TRAILER COACHES

"M" SYSTEM MFG. CO.
VICKSBURG
MISS.

ROYAL

ROYAL COACH CO.   HASTINGS. MICH.

LAKEWOOD
INDUSTRIES
ARTESIA, CALIF.

Continental
TRAILER COMPANY
CHICAGO

Quality
KIT
Mark

CENTURY
CUSTOM
BUILT
FEDERAL
TRAILER CO
DETROIT

GLIDER
TRAILER
CHICAGO, ILLINOIS
PATENTS PENDING

Lighthouse
TRAILER CO.
CHICAGO

LIBERTY
CARAVAN
COMFORT CONDITIONED SYSTEM
LICENSED UNDER SPENCER PATENTS   U.S. PATENT NO 2.225.244   OTHER PATENTS PENDING
LIBERTY COACH CO., INC.   BREMEN, INDIANA

TRAVELEZE
TRAILER CO.
BURBANK, CALIF.
SERIAL NO. 4815

CASSOPOLIS
MICHIGAN
WEST-WOOD
PRODUCTS
INC.

new
moon

The mighty loaf of bread! What better symbol of America could you pick to model a trailer after? OK, so maybe they didn't really use it as a model, but there were thousands of these handsome trailers produced from the thirties into the early fifties.

27 ft. Tandem

Cooler in Summer

Warmer in Winter

LIBERTY Trailers are Completely Furnished

When you inspect any model of a LIBERTY trailer, you'll be delighted with the top-quality furnishings that are featured throughout. Only the best beds, mattresses and springs, furniture, and kitchen equipment are included.

The "27" gives you a smart, modern mobile home

IF YOU select a LIBERTY "27," you will have a completely furnished, mobile, three-room apartment, offering every modern comfort and convenience essential to gracious living. You may choose a *full-size shower and flush toilet*, as well as a gas range, electric refrigerator, and hot-water heater, plus many other up-to-the-minute features if you make the family-size LIBERTY "27" your new trailer. The large double bed and studio couch provide sleeping accommodations for four.

"Butch and I love Dad's LIBERTY Trailer. Now we can play in the fresh air and sunshine."

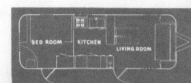

BED ROOM — KITCHEN — LIVING ROOM

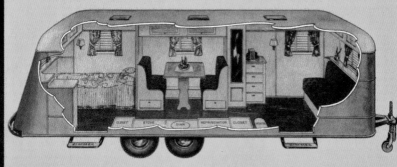

21 - 25 - 27 - 29 - 31 *Foot*

UNIVERSAL

Trailer Corporation

Chicago 4884 No. Clark St.   Los Angeles 15220 So. Lakewood Blvd.

The humble canned ham, a mainstay of the American kitchen and the most popular trailer shape of them all. With its flat sides and rounded bow and stern, these little gems were cheap to build, and dozens of manufacturers sprung up to meet the demands of the returning GIs who, after WWII, were hungry for a little family-friendly adventure. These are still as popular as ever, and when one pulls into a campground you can bet a crowd will soon appear.

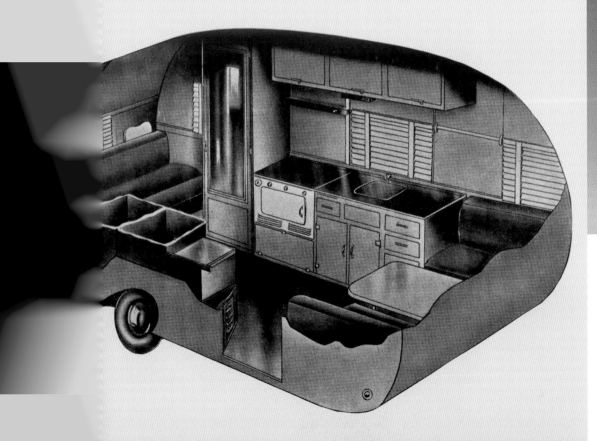

TINI HOME

Write today for complete details on the 12-foot Roomette (illustrated), 16-foot Tini Home and the 25-foot Suburban Home.

tini home
COACH COMPANY
ADDISON, ILLINOIS

VACATIONERS

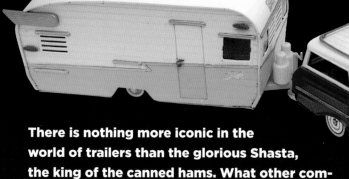

There is nothing more iconic in the world of trailers than the glorious Shasta, the king of the canned hams. What other company would have the audacity to put wings on their trailers? Collectors go nuts for these beauties and the name is spoken in hushed tones around the campfire.

24

The living room, the sitting room, the parlor, the den . . . all of these are wrapped up into one lovely little package in the trailer. It's where we visit and play cards and have our cocktails, and it's where we put up the Christmas tree or birthday decorations. Just like a house, the "front room" is where we do most of our living, and at night, as a bonus, the couch folds out into a comfy bed.

EVERY COMFORT... EVERY CONVENIENCE... EVERY FACILITY... FOR GRACIOUS AND ENJOYABLE LIVING

Fig. 2. Pleasant Living.

Many trailers sport what our family calls the "nook" or the "dinette": two opposing benches with a table in the middle. It's a great place to play cards, have a meal or just hang out. The kids can do their homework here while mom cooks dinner. Nothing's better than having your morning coffee while you look out on another glorious day from the comfort of your nook.

Cooking in a trailer may not always be the easiest thing in the world, and if you fry up that fresh-caught trout you will be smelling it for the next week. But trailer kitchens are a true marvel of ingenuity. Borrowing from the age-old traditions of boatbuilders, they have all the modern conveniences, often utilizing full-size appliances. I have seen people cook entire Thanksgiving meals in the modest kitchen of a 16-foot trailer.

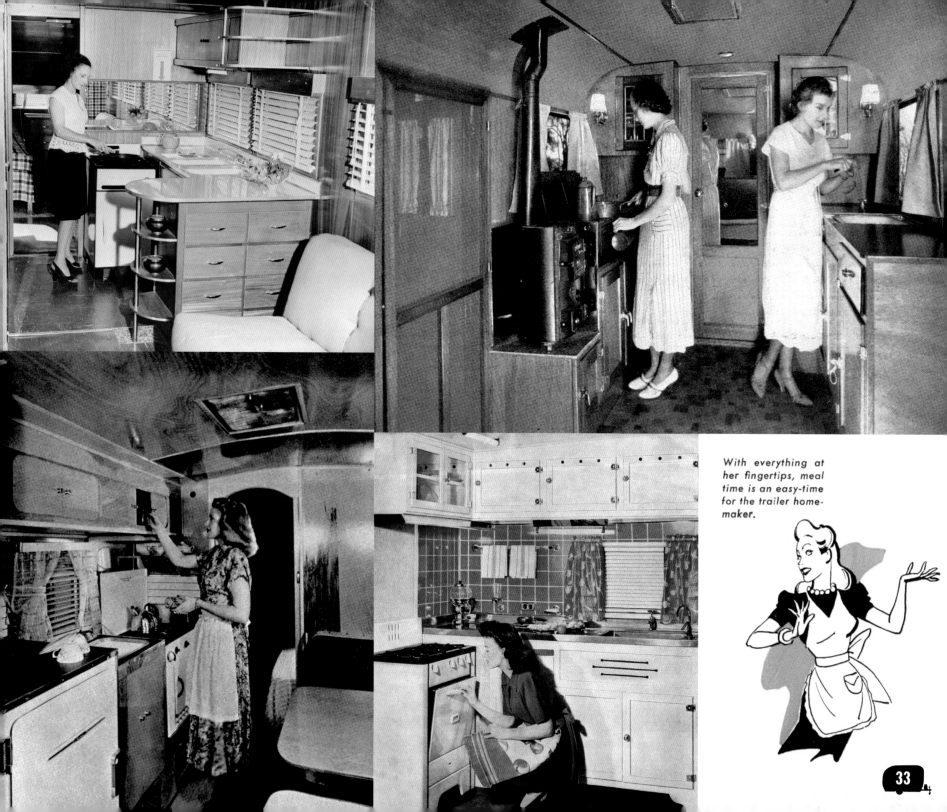

With everything at her fingertips, meal time is an easy-time for the trailer home-maker.

Meal Time

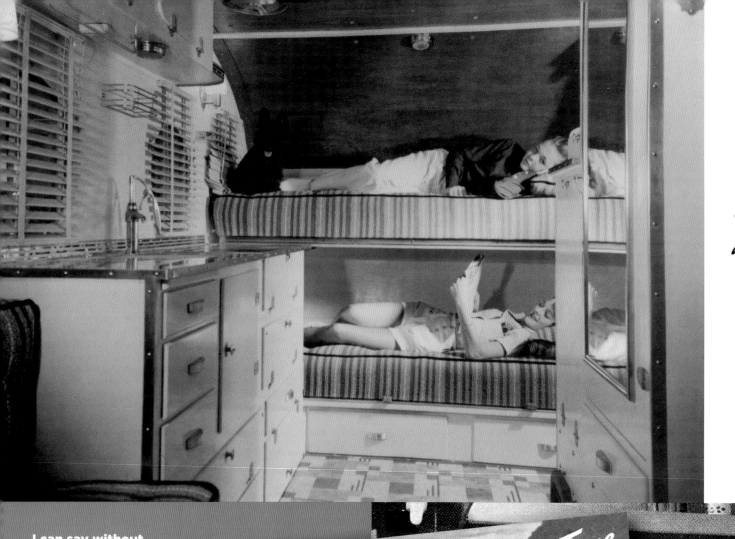

I can say without a doubt that a night spent in a trailer can be the coziest night of your life . . . and if you throw in some rain, forget about it!

Bed Time

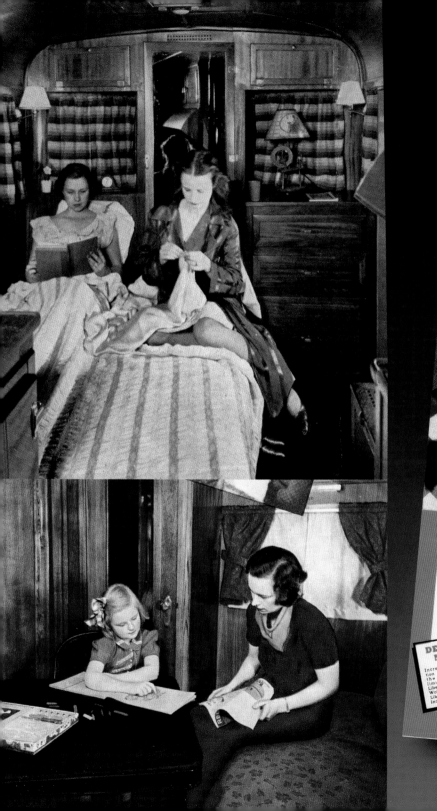

37

Like anything else in American pop culture, the trailer has been the subject of many songs over the years, and never was it more popular than in the 1930s—the golden age of trailering. Here are three examples, and for you ukulele players out there, the chords for "Little Trailer Town" are F, G^7, C^7, F^7 and B-flat^7. Have fun!

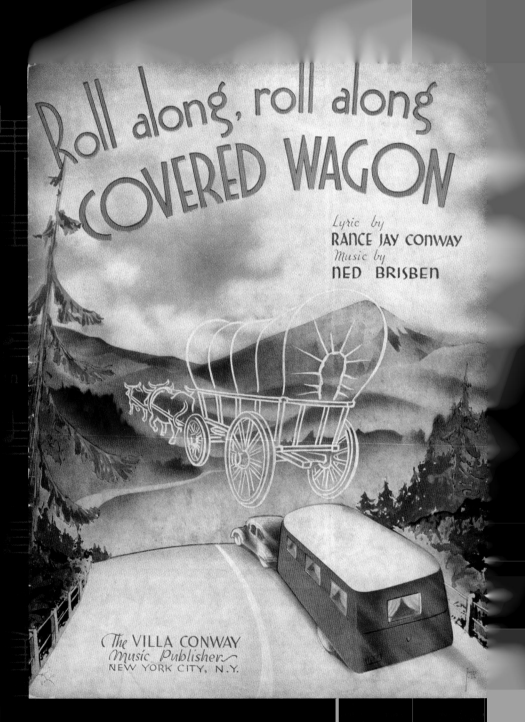

The allure of taking your home with you was not lost on the Hollywood crowd. In an industry where the phrase "hurry up and wait" is the motto, the ability to have a comfortable place to hang out was a must. From Eugene Pallette's "Cowboy Bunkhouse" to Barbara Stanwyck's "Shanty," the stars always had a home away from home, and cranky starlets could declare, "I'll be in my trailer!"

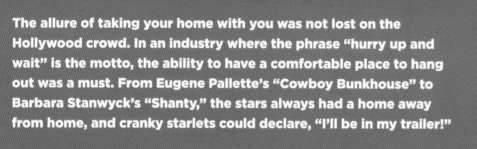

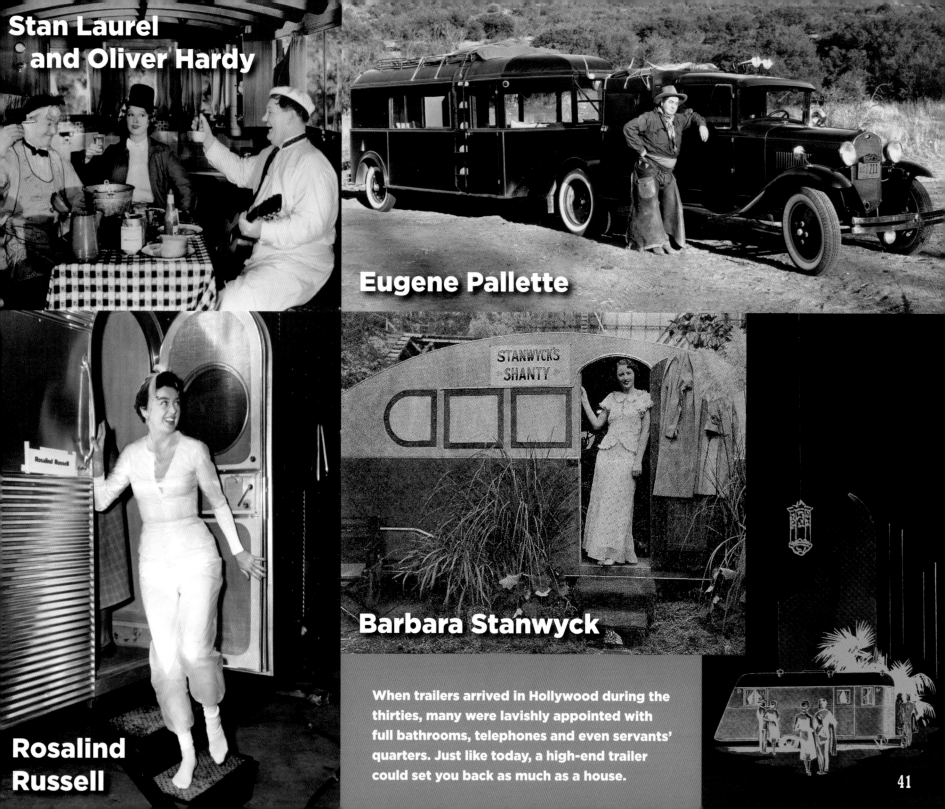

Stan Laurel and Oliver Hardy

Eugene Pallette

Rosalind Russell

STANWYCK'S SHANTY

Barbara Stanwyck

When trailers arrived in Hollywood during the thirties, many were lavishly appointed with full bathrooms, telephones and even servants' quarters. Just like today, a high-end trailer could set you back as much as a house.

41

Go Chase Yourself (1938) revolves around some bank robbers who jump in the trailer of some unsuspecting tourists. *The Covered Trailer* (1939) finds the Higgins family on a cross-country adventure after their South American cruise gets cancelled. Lots of trailer antics ensue!

Illustrierte film-Bühne

Nr. 2566

VILLA mit 100 PS

(THE LONG LONG TRAILER)

The Long, Long Trailer is the holy grail of trailer films. Released in 1953 and starring Lucille Ball and Desi Arnaz as Nicky and Tacy Collini, the plot revolves around the newlyweds buying a brand new forty-foot New Moon trailer to take on their honeymoon, and eventually around the country to engineering projects that Nicky is employed on. From hair-raising mountain passes, to tire changes on a muddy road and Tacy trying to cook while the trailer is moving, it's Desi and Lucy at their best. The film was a box office smash!

Selected as
America's Outstanding
Mobile Apartment Home

TO BE FEATURED IN

"THE LONG, LONG TRAILER"

STARRING

★ *LUCILLE BALL & DESI ARNAZ* ★

Color by
Technicolor

AN M-G-M PRODUCTION

Sherry Jackson

Ida Lupino

In the early days of Hollywood, actresses had to "rough it" while on location. With the introduction of trailers, they could have a comfortable place to change, rest and entertain. Photographers also had a new location to take the always-important publicity still.

June Lang

Jayne Mansfield

TRAVELING IN COMFORT—
No cramped riding for Ida Lupino when she goes vagabonding about by automobile on week-end trips. The blond Paramount ingenue has bought herself a silver streamlined trailer with all the comforts of home, including two convertible double beds, miniature kitchen sink, radio, card table and telephone connecting with the car ahead.

Hoot Gibson

W. C. Fields

Gary Cooper

While many actors were introduced to trailers on the set, they quickly realized how convenient they were for life on the road. W. C. Fields had a rolling men's club custom built, with the bar being the focal point. And writer Erle Stanley Gardner had a fleet for himself and his secretaries so he could always be working while traveling.

Wallace Beery

Eddie Cantor

Ginger Rogers and husband Jack Briggs

Ginger Rogers was a true champion for the trailer, and she even had a two-story Liberty that cranked up and down. This model was not a success, as it would tend to blow over in heavy winds. The caption on this photo of Gypsy Rose Lee reads, "The Mayor of Paradise Cove Trailer Park, in the yard of her canopied trailer home." The Malibu park is still there, and the Hollywood elite are happy to pay over a million dollars just to purchase a trailer to live in a trailer park.

Gypsy Rose Lee

SEPTEMBER 1937
A.N.C.

Trailer Travel
MAGAZINE

Combining TRAILER LIFE

★

In This Issue

What Is Happening to the Trailer Industry?
KARL HALE DIXON

Trailerite Associations Turn Faces Toward Future
CARL W. MASON—AL J. SWEENEY

Hollywood Takes to Trailers . . . .
EDISON R. HARRIS

Westward Ho! . . . . . .
R. T. PETTIT, M.D.

Housekeeping on Wheels Touring Guide . . . Sports Trailer Industry News

Loretta Young

15¢

ORIGINAL AND FOREMOST MAGAZINE IN AMERICA DEVOTED TO TRAILER INTERESTS

Queen for a Day

The Queen for a Day television program ran from 1956 to 1964 and featured host Jack Bailey giving away prizes to the most needy contestants. Clearly the trailer industry was happy to help.

Trailers worked their way into many Hollywood films, from the idyllic trailer honeymoon shared by Fredric March and Janet Gaynor in the original *A Star Is Born* (1937, left), to the trailer park Tony Perkins lives in to save money on his college expenses in *Tall Story* (1960, above). Even director King Vidor embraced the trailer as a mobile office to go over a scene with Karen Morley for *Our Daily Bread* (1934).

King Vidor and Karen Morley

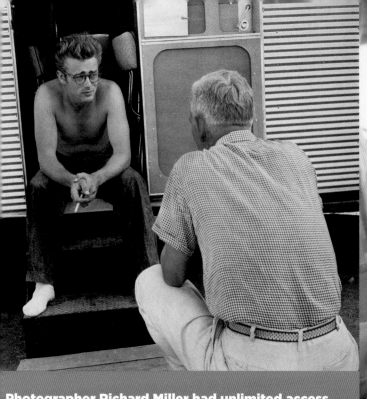

Photographer Richard Miller had unlimited access to the set of the iconic 1956 film *Giant*. These candid shots reveal a relaxed cast who clearly enjoyed hanging out in their Airfloat trailer with its corrugated aluminum exterior, ribbon mahogany woodwork and very unique porthole windows.

Rock Hudson, Elizabeth Taylor and James Dean

ket and skirt of royal red cashmere suede
are worn for traveling.

Rear view of skirt and jacket. The hat is
fashioned of royal red suede.

With the skirt discarded, the costume becomes a cool dress-and-cape outfit.

"Road Show"

**A New Trailer
Traveling Ensemble**

A trailer travel ensemble that combines
a traveling suit, a smart street outfit and
an informal evening gown is the triumph
of a designer in the Hal Roach movie
studios.

The basic tunic dress is fashioned of
non-crushable silk crepe in three shades
of blue. Over this is worn a jacket and
skirt of royal red cashmere suede. The
entire costume is washable and needs no
ironing.

With it is worn a jaunty little hat of
royal red suede. The pumps are royal
red kid finished with an Indian beaded
ornament.

A few deft motions and milady—as
shown here by Rosina Lawrence, the
lovely Hal Roach, M-G-M star—is prepared for any occasion en route!

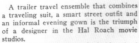

skirt and jacket removed, the silk dress
becomes a full-length evening gown.

For sunning and bathing during her trailer
outings, Della Lind, who appears in M-G-M's
"Rosalie," selects this sunwaher, bathing

Designs for Living in a Trailer

Simple, practical clothes like the designs shown on these pages are ideal for trailer travel. Easy to make and comfortable to wear, they will solve your vacation needs. See pages 50 and 54 for further descriptions by Alice Hutton

Turban 7393

Crownless Turban 7393

7423 Well-cut, well-pressed slacks and shirt. For 36 (size 18), 2¾ yards 35-inch sail-cloth; 2 yards 35-inch cotton. 12 to 20; 30 to 40. 25 Cents.

Butterick Pattern 7380

Butterick Pattern 7352

7380 For stop-offs, a shirt-dress, with a gored skirt, a yoke. For 36 (size 18), 3¼ yards 35-inch printed cotton. yards 39-inch striped acetate. Sizes 12 to 20; 30 to 44. 45 cts.

7352 A pleated-skirt shirt-frock. For 36 (size 18), 4½ 12 to 20; 30 to 46. 45 Cts. Tur-ban 7393, 21½ to 23. 25 Cts.

7382 Tucks on the pockets, mono sleeves. For 36 (size 18), 3¼ yards 39-in. rayon crepe. 12 to 20; 30 to 44. 45 Cents.

7371 Envelope-fold kimono inverted below the yoke, ki-sleeves for this. For 36 (size 18), 3⅛ yards 39-inch print. 12 to 20; 30 to 42. 45 Cts. Tur-ban 7393, 21½ to 23. 25 Cents.

E

D

Butterick Pattern 7382

Butterick Pattern 7371

Butterick Pattern 5990

Butterick Pattern 7185

7185 Time off for a sun-bath in classic-cut shorts, stitch-trimmed shirt. For 36 (size 18), 3 yards 35-inch linen. Sizes 12 to 20; 30 to 40. 25 Cts.

5990 Out of bed and into pa-jamas, one-piece, tailored, wide-trousered. For 36 (size 18), 4¾ yards 35-inch printed pique. Sizes 12 to 20; 30 to 44. 35 Cts.

7383 Slacks, a halter, and a bolero for morning. For 36 (size 18), 4¼ yards 35-inch linen; ¾ yard 35-inch print. 12 to 20; 30 to 40. 40 Cents.

Butterick Pattern 7383

A

B

Butterick Pattern 7423

Butterick Patterns Can Be Purchased At Leading Stores and Shops Anywhere

Sept. 15 1934

THE NEW YORKER

Price 20 cts.

Garrett Price

These days the trailer sometimes gets a bad name, and the words "trailer trash" get bandied about quite a bit. But early on, the travel trailer garnered much more respect, and was actually considered a toy for the rich, as a new trailer could set you back the price of a new home. These magazine covers are a testament to the mighty travel trailer.

The Saturday Evening

POST

February 2, 1952 • 15¢

TRAILER PARK
OFFICE

JOHN & LIZZIE
WILSON
BOSTON, MASS.

TEXACO Oasis

Why it pays you to travel light!

WHEN YOU TRAVEL with luggage made of aluminum you not only get paid off in lightness... but also in matchless *beauty*, plus strength that can withstand the roughest treatment. No other material offers such a unique *combination* of advantages. Which is the reason why Kaiser Aluminum is now being used in thousands of new products!

HOUSE TRAILERS of Kaiser Aluminum give you an accountable pay-off. With needless dead weight eliminated, you spend less on tires and fuel. Maintenance problems on your trailer disappear. And its beauty can't be marred by rust. These advantages explain why dollar-smart *commercial* operators use trucks built of Kaiser Aluminum!

CANOES, ROWBOATS, small craft of every description, are now being made of Kaiser Aluminum. And here again, Kaiser Aluminum pays off in lightness, strength, maintenance-free beauty. No wonder thousands of manufacturers who are looking for extra sales appeal are looking to Kaiser Aluminum... for the top-notch quality you demand!

For another dependable source... choose

Kaiser Aluminum

product of Permanente Metals Corp.

FOR NAMES OF MANUFACTURERS MAKING THE PRODUCTS PICTURED ABOVE, WRITE: PERMANENTE PRODUCTS COMPANY, DEPT. P-9, CONSUMER SERVICE DIVISION, KAISER BLDG., OAKLAND 12, CALIF.

PAY-OFF FOR MANUFACTURERS

The *saleability* of Kaiser Aluminum should be reason enough to consider using it in your product. But that's not all...

Consider, for example, the ease with which it can be fabricated—that it can be formed, drawn, spun, brazed, welded. That it can be painted or polished, or finished in almost any way. That it saves costs on fabricating, handling, shipping.

Then consider that with Kaiser Aluminum you assure yourself *consistent* quality... plus the services of an organization noted for dependable deliveries. Aren't these reasons enough for investigating Kaiser Aluminum—today?

The trailer has always represented mobility, adventure and, in the early days, elegance. What better subject to help sell your products?

Your car + trailer needs gas + ETHYL

At pumps marked "Ethyl" you get *four* values:

1 More anti-knock fluid (containing lead tetraethyl) than you get in the best regular-grade gasoline. That means more power.

2 All-round quality (including quick starting) that is *double-tested*—by the oil company and by the Ethyl Gasoline Corporation.

3 100% performance from your high compression engine.

4 Saving on oil as well as gas by preventing knock and overheating.

NEXT TIME GET ETHYL... A BETTER RUN FOR YOUR MONEY

FOR THE BEST VACATION WITH YOUR TRAILER
Come to Michigan!

Wonderful highways-good roads and intriguing trails lead you to innumerable places by lake or stream where you may go with your trailer. 74 State Parks from 12 to 15,000 acres - all conveniences and playground equip 1,500,000 acres National Forests—numerous State Forests.

Send Stamps for STATE MAP and 76 page GUIDE

BOX A
EAST MICHIGAN TOURIST ASS'N
BAY CITY, MICHIGAN

WHEN YOU'RE SNUGLY PARKED...
but you gotta go!

on errands, for instance:

There's nothing handier than an easily-and-snugly portable Folding COMPAX bike for errands or short jaunts about the country . . . for exercise to keep you trim!

Extra sturdy, this handy Columbia-built bicycle folds into practically no space at all—weighs little—makes an ideal trailer companion.

You need no tools to set it up or take it apart. It's so simple a child can do it, in a mere matter of minutes!

It has only two simple points of assembly: handlebars and super-strong reinforced frame joints—so sturdy it was used by paratroopers!

For Healthful Exercise
Trailer-tripping sometimes cheats folks of needed exercise. Cycling provides the best of exercise and fun too: for the whole family.

Write for free literature with full information on COMPAX and many other bikes by Columbia today!

A Quality Product of America's Oldest Bicycle Manufacturers

ILLUSTRATED is the lightweight COMPAX "Sports Traveler", with lightweight tires, coaster brake, adjustable saddle and handlebars, chain guard and kick stand. In red, blue, or black with gold striping. All three Columbia-built beauties

COMPAX by *Columbia*

THE WESTFIELD MANUFACTURING COMPANY
116 CYCLE STREET, WESTFIELD, MASSACHUSETTS
SINCE 1877... AMERICA'S FIRST BICYCLE
June, 1949   61

Thanks to Sir Thomas,
even a Queen has nothing on Mrs. Jones!

Sir Thomas Lipton was official "Tea Merchant By Appointment" to three different Royal Families. But his famous tea can be enjoyed by Mrs. Jones, Mrs. Smith, Mrs. Tom, Dick, and Harry.

For anyone, everyone, can afford the best, due to the happy fact that today tea—even a tea as fine as Lipton's—costs less than any other beverage except water!

1. No one did more to bring down the price of tea than Sir Thomas Lipton. When he entered the business, he found hold-over ideas from days when tea was known only to royal lips and $50 a pound was a not unusual price.

2. Sir Thomas pioneered in the scientific cultivation and blending of tea. And besides developing a tea flavor finer than the world had ever known, he also worked out ways to grow tea for less . . to ship, handle and sell it for less.

3. So today, even though this famous tea merchant was honored by royalty . . . even though his tea is known in America and in six other leading tea-drinking nations as "the world's most delicious" . . . it is within the reach of everyone. It's the largest selling tea in the world.

LIPTON'S TEA

4. Buy a package of Lipton's from your grocer today. Brew a clear, rich, inviting cup. As its enticing aroma arises and its delicious flavor warms you, you will understand why five great World's Fairs awarded top honors to Lipton's Tea . . . why the Great Tea Exposition of Ceylon and India proclaimed tea from Sir Thomas' own gardens "The Choicest Tea Grown"

The characters Mrs. Jones and Mrs. Smith are fictitious and represent no actual persons.

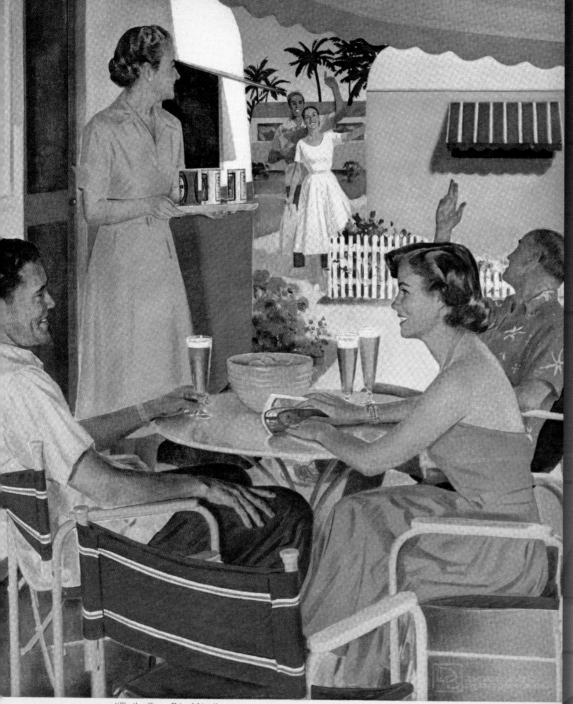

"Trailer Camp Friendships," by Douglass Crockwell. Number 79 in the series "Home Life in America"

this friendly, freedom-loving land of ours—Beer belongs . . . enjoy it!

BEER AND ALE—AMERICA'S BEVERAGES OF MODERATION
Sponsored by the United States Brewers Foundation . . . Chartered 1862

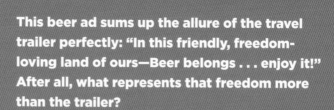

This beer ad sums up the allure of the travel trailer perfectly: "In this friendly, freedom-loving land of ours—Beer belongs . . . enjoy it!" After all, what represents that freedom more than the trailer?

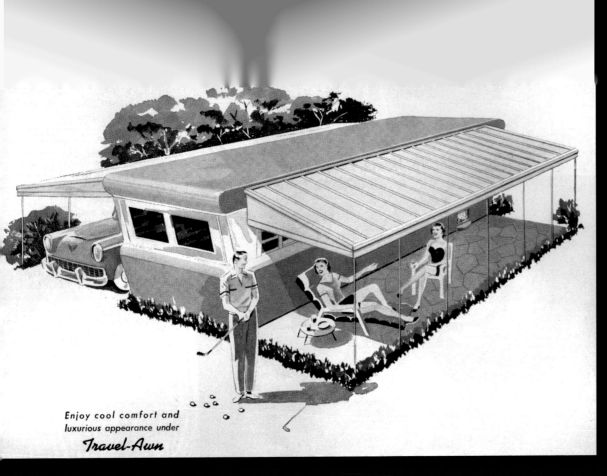

Enjoy cool comfort and luxurious appearance under

Travel-Awn

Parts & Accessories

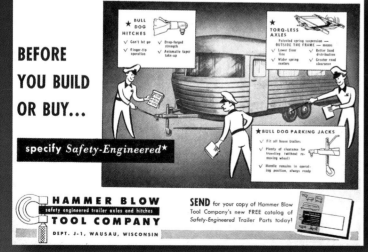

Trailers and romance? You bet! Couples and trailers are a perfect pairing. There is nothing like images of happy couples to help sell your product, whether curled up in the cozy interior or enjoying the view from their beautiful campsite.

Even away out WEST they sing their praise of ELCAR!

Everywhere you go it's Elcar—Elcar—Elcar. The thousands of Elcars out in use are daily selling more Elcars. Dependability—size—beauty—added conveniences—value each important, but when combined, the result is an Elcar. So why shouldn't owners be praising the Elcar Trailer. You, too, want all the important advantages, and Elcar gives them to you at no extra cost.

For good looks, for roomy comfort, and for down-right quality engineering you can't touch the new 1941 Elcars, even in lots of trailers sold at much higher prices. See your Elcar dealer or send for catalog today.

ELCAR COACH COMPANY, INC.
Dept. AT-6—Elkhart, Indiana

"Elcar is one of the fastest selling trailers ever made. Examine it, compare it. You'll see why!"

What's manlier than a cowboy? There seems to be a plethora of ads featuring cowboys. Were they for the benefit of the men or the ladies?

THE *BEST* BRAND IN TEXAS
MOBILE SCOUT

MODELS 13, 15, 16, 17 and 20. MODELS 16, 17 AND 20 ARE SELF-CONTAINED UNITS. BIRCH INTERIOR, ICE BOX OR BUTANE REFRIGERATOR, MORE WINDOWS, MORE AIR. IT IS TRAILER ENGINEERED, TRAVEL TESTED, FIBERGLASS INSULATED, STORAGE FOR ALL THE FAMILY AND IT TRAILS LIKE A SHADOW.

Write for descriptive brochure and name of nearest dealer.

MOBILE SCOUT INC.
2110 WEST DIVISION   ARLINGTON, TEXAS
Telephone: CRestview 4-5153

APPROVED
TRAILER COACHES
Offer You the Best in Travel Comfort

ENJOY the thrilling independence... the welcome ECONOMY... of taking your own private living quarters with you! Approved trailer coaches— built to basic standards of T.C.M.A. by the leaders of the industry—are preferred by thousands for extra utility and convenience, years of satisfaction, and utmost dollar value. Write today for free illustrated book about America's finest trailer coaches, manufactured by T.C.M.A. members.

MORE AND BETTER PARKS

Housing the substantial citizens who patronize good trailer parks is BIG business. In addition to the hundreds now in operation there is an excellent profit opportunity for one in your community. T.C.M.A. will give you valuable facts and guidance in establishing a profitable park, even to free architect's plans and the specific advice of full-time experts retained by the Association.

Write for "Planning a Profitable Trailer Park." This free booklet contains a wealth of pictures, diagrams and cost data. Address Trailer Parks Div., Department 219, Trailer Coach Manufacturers Assn. Civic Opera Building, Chicago 6, Illinois.

T.C.M.A. APPROVED TRAILER COACHES

GLIDER • HOOSIER-RAMBLER • HOWARD • INDIAN IRONWOOD • KIT • LA SALLE • LIBERTY • LIGHTHOUSE LUXOR • MACOMB • MAIN-LINE • MODERN • NATIONAL PALACE • PAN AMERICAN • PLATT • PRAIRIE SCHOONER ROYCRAFT • SCHULT • SPORTSMAN • STREAMLITE • STEWART TRAVELITE • TRAVELO • TROTWOOD • UNIVERSAL VAGABOND • WALCO • WHITLEY • ZIMMER • ADAMS ALL-STATES • AMERICAN • COLUMBIA • CONTINENTAL CONWAY • DREXLER • DUO • ELCAR • GENERAL

TRAILER COACH
Mfrs. Assn.

North—East—West—South—wherever there's a Travelo—there's lasting comfort
and security—AND a friendly Travelo dealer, ready to serve you.

Wherever you go--the sign you know—

TRAVELO

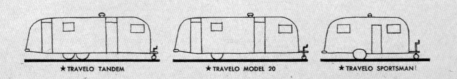

★ TRAVELO TANDEM   ★ TRAVELO MODEL 20   ★ TRAVELO SPORTSMAN

Travelo . . . Manufactured by Raymond Products Co., Inc., Saginaw, Michigan

Vacation NEWS by **SILVER DOME**

It's bigger...
easier to
live in...
it's the *new*

STAR

★ Your newest, biggest value in trailer living . . . lightweight, quality built, economy priced

· TROTWOOD ·
The Ideal Trailer for Your Traveling Home

You're always "at home" with a TROTWOOD—anytime, anywhere. On long vacations or week-end trips it's so easy to hitch the lightweight, easy towing TROTWOOD "ECONOMY" Model to your car and enjoy carefree travel and fun. Light and compactly built, yet plenty of room for four persons. Beautifully finished and affording every convenience. THE LOWEST PRICED QUALITY TRAILER. Backed by 18 years of trailer-building experience, and the 9th successful year of the Economy model. Write for Illustrated literature to Department Y B47

TROTWOOD TRAILERS, INC.   TROTWOOD, OHIO

ALWAYS TRAVEL WITH A TROTWOOD

TROTWOOD
WITH NEW BEAUTY INSIDE AND OUT!

Priced from $980. Completely equipped, including electric brakes and Fed. tax. THREE MODELS to choose from, 17½ ft., 18 ft. 8 in., and 22 ft. 5 in. A TROTWOOD is your guarantee of: 1—Quality construction throughout. 2—Long life. 3—Low first and maintenance cost. 4—Superior road performance. 5—A trailer coach built by one of oldest manufacturers in the industry. Write today for literature and name of nearest TROTWOOD dealer.

TROTWOOD TRAILERS, INC., 89 Main St., TROTWOOD, OHIO

Trotwood had great ads! Whomever they hired to do their pen-and-ink drawings was a genius. With the advent of the digital age, that's something we don't see much anymore, which is a shame. There is a warmth and elegance to these images, and nobody did it better than Trotwood.

Return Postage Guaranteed
TROTWOOD TRAILERS INC.
Trotwood, Ohio

TROTWOOD TRAILERS
"Travel with a Trotwood"

The "CUB"

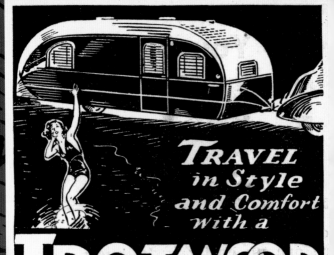

TRAVEL in Style and Comfort with a

TROTWOOD

CUSTOM-BUILT

In any climate — under any road conditions TROTWOOD Engineering offers the utmost in Safety, Individuality, Beauty-of-line and Interior Appointments. Unsurpassed for permanent living quarters, extended travel or short vacation. 7 different models to choose from, starting at $315 equipped. *Wire. write or call for new Trailer Book. Address,*

Trotwood Trailers, Inc.
108 Main St., TROTWOOD, OHIO
5 Miles N. W. of Dayton, Ohio

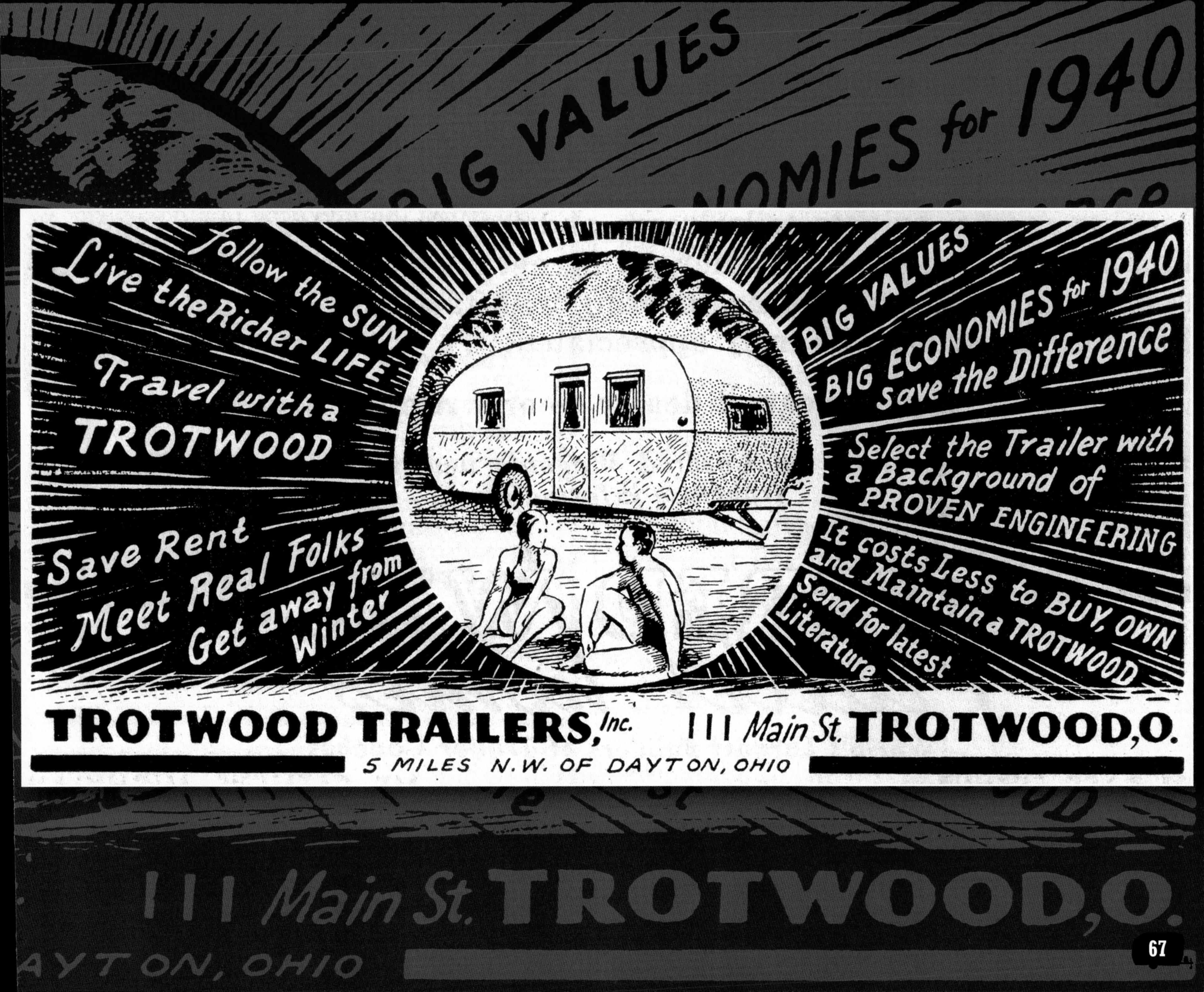
follow the SUN
Live the Richer LIFE
Travel with a
TROTWOOD
Save Rent
Meet Real Folks
Get away from
Winter
BIG VALUES
BIG ECONOMIES for 1940
Save the Difference
Select the Trailer with
a Background of
PROVEN ENGINEERING
It costs Less to BUY, OWN
and Maintain a TROTWOOD
Send for latest
Literature
TROTWOOD TRAILERS, Inc.
111 Main St. TROTWOOD, O.
5 MILES N.W. OF DAYTON, OHIO

Trail R News

NEWS • TEST REPORTS • TRAVEL • PERSONALITIES

AUGUST, 1953 • 20c

Trailerocracy

Felices Fiesta

Poor Man's Game Bird

The old adage "sex sells" was certainly as pertinent to the trailer industry as it was to the rest of the advertising world. Beautiful models were always a bonus while trying to peddle your product. Not sure about the gent showing the lovely ladies the trailer model . . . he looks like a wolf!

Trail -R- News

Devoted to the Exclusive Interest of All Trailerit

The All-inclusive Trailer Coach Journa

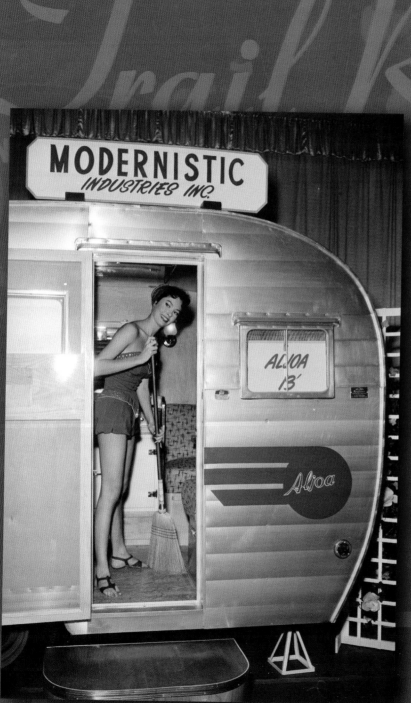

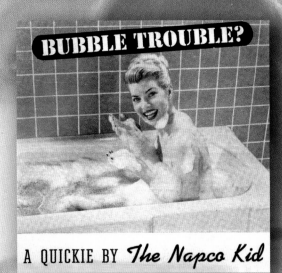

BUBBLE TROUBLE?

A QUICKIE BY *The Napco Kid*

It's a funny thing . . . I have page after page of advertising featuring beautiful women in various stages of bathing. The great thing is how big they make the bathrooms look in these images. As anybody who has ever taken a shower in a vintage trailer can attest, it's a bit like showering in a phone booth.

Next time choose LIBERTY...

have all the conveniences of a modern home!

When you select LIBERTY, you choose completely modern living. Showers and flush toilets, plus most up-to-the-minute conveniences may be a part of your new LIBERTY Trailer. Do not delay. See the new, completely furnished LIBERTY Trailers at an AUTHORIZED LIBERTY DEALER today. And remember! LIBERTY Trailers are designed for living and driving comfort

Only Liberty Offers Comfort-Conditioning

Forced-draft heating and "attic" ventilation combine to keep the temperature in each room pleasant and comfortable in any climate. In winter, cold air is drawn off the floor, heated, and forced beneath. Constant air circulation through the "attic" keeps the trailer cooler in summer.

Dealers Note:

Increased production facilities allow the addition of a limited number of Liberty dealerships. Write C. K. Kinder, Liberty Coach Co., Inc., Bremen, Ind.

SEE AN AUTHORIZED DEALER TODAY!

Liberty

America's Foremost Trailer

LIBERTY COACH CO., INC.
Bremen, Indiana

71

"You get a full-size bath with shower stall and all the conveniences of a modern apartment."

AIRSTREAM TRAILERS

There is no other trailer company more iconic than Airstream. It is the Harley-Davidson of the trailer world, and rightfully so. After tinkering in his garage for a few years, Airstream founder Wally Byam went into full production in 1932, and the company is still going strong. Airstreams didn't always look like the silver bullets we know today; the Torpedo, Silver Cloud and Airlite came first. Many of Wally's early trailers were do-it-yourself kits made out of Masonite.

The Airstream
1938

Airstreamers put a lot of love into keeping their rigs highly polished. If you have ever had the pleasure of seeing one parked by the ocean at sunset with the golden light reflecting off the aluminum, you will never forget it.

Tent trailers and teardrops are not just second cousins to the full-size travel trailer; they belong at the same table at family dinners. In fact, the very first travel trailers were homemade and used canvas for walls. The teardrop was an affordable and easy tow alternative to the comparatively massive trailers that required a big V8 to get you down the road. There is a passionate community of collectors who revere the teardrop in all its pint-sized wonder.

This very early example of a homemade tent trailer used what looks like a wagon chassis. As it has four wooden-spoked wheels, it must not have sped down the road, but it sure beat sleeping on the ground. It was contraptions like this that helped start the travel trailer craze.

1. Select a pleasant campsite with plenty of shade and grass.

2. Lower body legs and adjust to proper height. Remove tarpaulin cover.

3. Unbuckle body straps and remove grooved molding from bedsprings.

4. Fold out both bedsprings with all bedding strapped in position.

5. Place tent framework in position in sockets on trailer body.

6. Place ridge and upright poles in tent and swing to vertical position.

7. Carry tent over framework at sides and draw grommets over pins.

8. Tie canvas back to form door opening and hang netting in position under flap.

**Home life in camp. Neighbors join the campfire circle—
"One touch of nature makes the whole world kin."
—William Shakespeare**

The Auto-Kamp Trailer Model No. 4 is Large, Roomy and Comfortable

The Roomy double Beds are 38 inches off the ground.
The Floor between is High and Dry.
The large dressing space 48 x 78 inches has ample head room.

A Storage Space is provided under each bed.

Note the always accessible ice box and food compartment, the convenient step and large doorway.

The Split Coach was a marvel of ingenuity, and once it was set up you had a very roomy space indeed. This was the precursor to the pop-outs you see on modern trailers. The average salary in the United States in 1930 was just over $1,300, so you can see that the Split Coach was a serious investment.

And Now A NEW LUXURIOUS TYPE *of* TRANSPORTATION

SPLIT COACH

THE COMPANION CAR TO ALL CARS

No wider than a motor car BUT— *it pulls out like an accordion.*

Opens up like an umbrella AND — *becomes wider than a railway train.*

A CHAMPION OF AUTOMOTIVE DESIGN

These pictures portray the DeLuxe Split Coach. The Standard Model is the same but its equipment is slightly modified and its trimmings are not as lavish.

The extraordinary devices contained in Split Coach function during the traveling condition and also during the parked or "split" state. This is an outstanding feature; for if it were necessary to split the vehicle in order to use the equipment contained therein, its utility would be considerably curtailed.

Patents pending in U. S., Canada and seven foreign countries.

STANDARD $875.

DE LUXE $1250.

Split Coach provides the greatest expansion ever given to a vehicle. In its expanded state, the vehicle becomes approximately three times larger than its normal size. It obviates hotel bills and meals in restaurants. It can be coupled to any make of motor car and trails with extraordinary ease.

Split Coach is designed to fill the entire traveling requirements of four persons. Whether mobile or stationary, Split Coach combines the comforts of a drawing room, dining room, bedroom, kitchen, bathroom with toilet conveniences, and dressing room. This is the maximum of comfort and utility at the minimum of cost.

· EXHIBITED · AT · THE · NATIONAL · SHOWS ·

THE COMPANION CAR TO ALL CARS

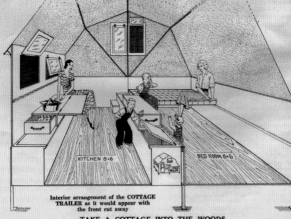

Interior arrangement of the COTTAGE TRAILER as it would appear with the front cut away

TAKE A COTTAGE INTO THE WOODS

The tent trailer was light, inexpensive and easy to set up, and sure beat a tent that you had to put on the ground. The interiors were surprisingly roomy. You could take the whole family camping and everybody had a comfy place to sleep.

TRAILCAMPER
Luxury Living for Campers and Tourists

All the family will glory in outdoor living in a convenient and comfortable TRAILCAMPER. Camp in the mountains—at the lake or seaside—travel where you will and be free of hotel or cabin worries. That's TRAILCAMPER living.

TRAILCAMPER offers spring beds with mattresses—for two to four people. High and dry—up off the ground. Cool and airy in hot weather—warm and cozy in cool climes.

Sturdy, all-steel long-life body that "hugs the road" without sideway, opens up in a jiffy to a spacious tent-room, with attached canopy. Fully screened—weather proof.

Goes anywhere your car can travel. No drag, easy on gas. Comes complete with stove, ice box, table, chairs, etc., ready for luxurious living on the road or in summer camp.

Write today for illustrated literature and name of nearest display.

DOR-LEE PRODUCTS CO.
S. Cornell and E. 75th St., Chicago 49, Ill.
Also Manufacturers of the famous TRAILSLEEPER

Some excellent dealerships still available

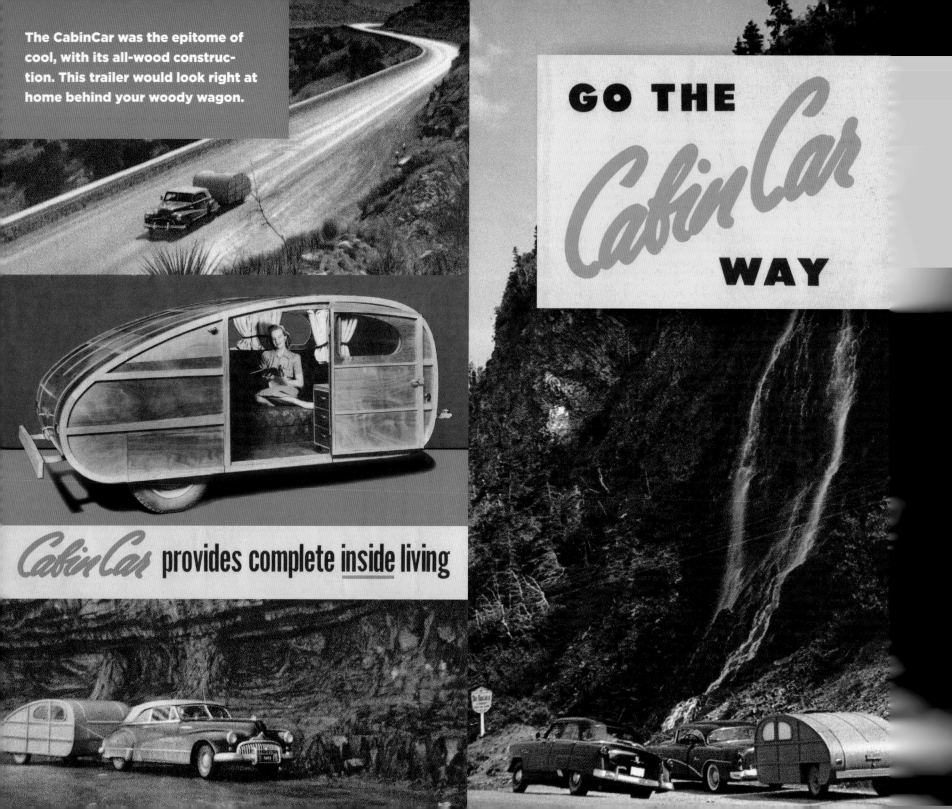

The CabinCar was the epitome of cool, with its all-wood construction. This trailer would look right at home behind your woody wagon.

GO THE *CabinCar* WAY

CabinCar provides complete **inside** living

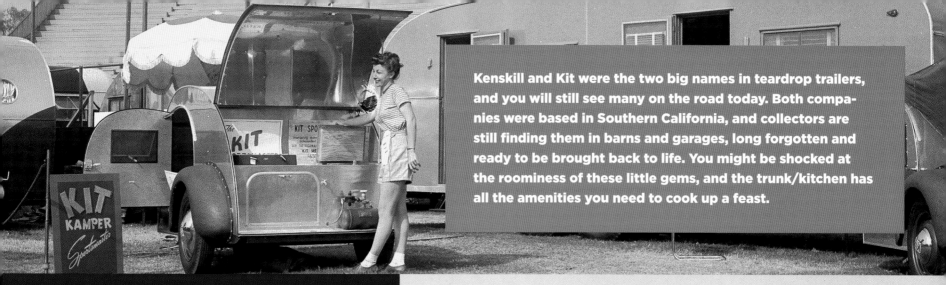

Kenskill and Kit were the two big names in teardrop trailers, and you will still see many on the road today. Both companies were based in Southern California, and collectors are still finding them in barns and garages, long forgotten and ready to be brought back to life. You might be shocked at the roominess of these little gems, and the trunk/kitchen has all the amenities you need to cook up a feast.

HIT THE FUN TRAIL in a KIT

Enjoy the best vacation you have ever had in solid comfort with a KIT. Sling your gear in a bag—hitch your KIT to the car and you're off. Two sleep snug in a KIT—no tent pitching—no damp bedding or mosquito slapping—just loads of comfort and fun. Complete kitchen facilities with stove, ice box, pantry, all in a trailer weighing less than 600 lbs. Two models to choose from: The KIT Kamper or the KIT Sportsmaster, priced within range of every sportsman and vacationer. Write for folder and name of nearest dealer.

National Distributors
SACKETT-NICHOLSON CORP.
2481 American Avenue
Long Beach, California

Produced by
Kit Manufacturing Co.
Norwalk, California

THE FAMOUS **KIT** TRAILERS

66

This beauty, a pop-up teardrop that cranks up from the side, is an anomaly that has stumped everybody I've shown these photos to. The awning off the back leads to a roomy canvas tent for your guests.

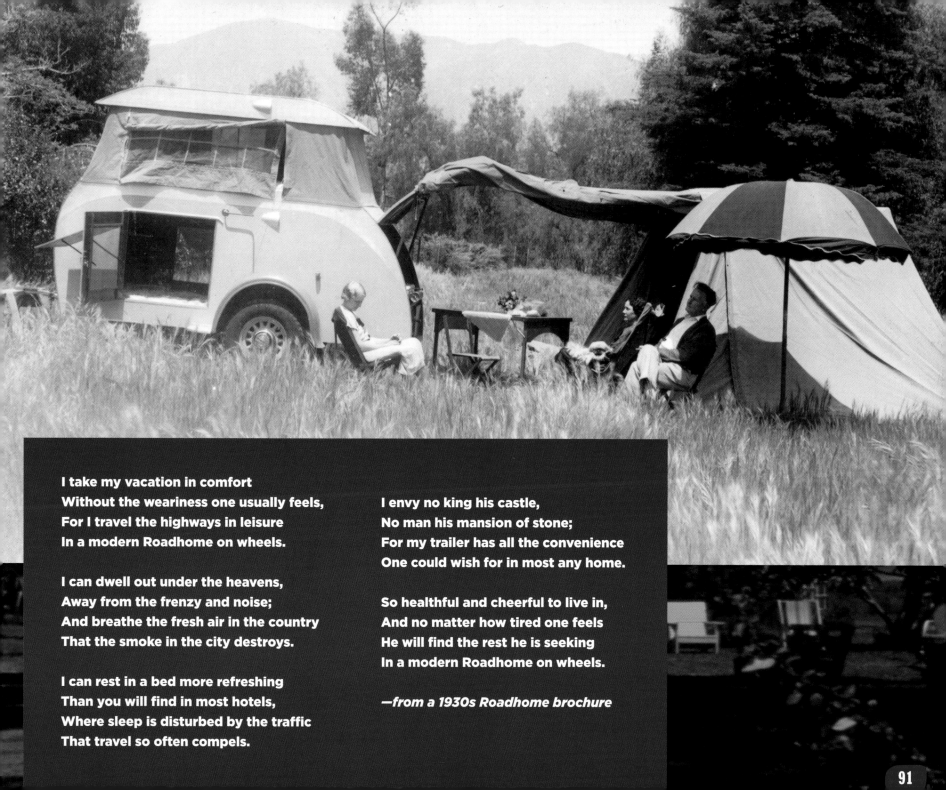

I take my vacation in comfort
Without the weariness one usually feels,
For I travel the highways in leisure
In a modern Roadhome on wheels.

I can dwell out under the heavens,
Away from the frenzy and noise;
And breathe the fresh air in the country
That the smoke in the city destroys.

I can rest in a bed more refreshing
Than you will find in most hotels,
Where sleep is disturbed by the traffic
That travel so often compels.

I envy no king his castle,
No man his mansion of stone;
For my trailer has all the convenience
One could wish for in most any home.

So healthful and cheerful to live in,
And no matter how tired one feels
He will find the rest he is seeking
In a modern Roadhome on wheels.

—from a 1930s Roadhome brochure

Step One:
Arrive at your campsite.

There have been all kinds of contraptions over the years that crank up, fold out and ultimately make something compact and easy to tow into a comfy home on wheels. The caption from one of these 1962 photos on this page says, "The entire unit can be readied for camping within five minutes." The Trailorboat (facing page) was built from 1961 to 1963, and is about as cool as it gets. Not only do you have a comfy place to sleep and cook your meals, but you have your boat along as well.

Step Two:
Turn this little doohickey.

Step Three:
Enjoy your cozy cottage!

Step One:
Arrive at your campsite.

Step Two: Get some guy to help with your cooler top.

Step Three: Your gal pal will help you hoist the boat.

Step Four:
All set for a row!

Meet Larry Shank . . . that's him with his mom and dad in the fifties in front of their 1947 Kenskill model 10 trailer that they bought used in 1952. After a lifetime of adventures, that trailer and the green Willys jeep are still being used by Larry, along with all the original camping gear and goodies. He is the envy of us all and is always happy to share his family's stories by the campfire.

Before the Internet and minimalls and shopping centers, businessmen had to hit the road to peddle their wares, and what better way to show off that shiny new washing machine or boat motor? The trailer, of course! People figured out that they could drag a lot of stuff behind their sedans and not have to rely on pictures or tiny salesman's samples anymore.

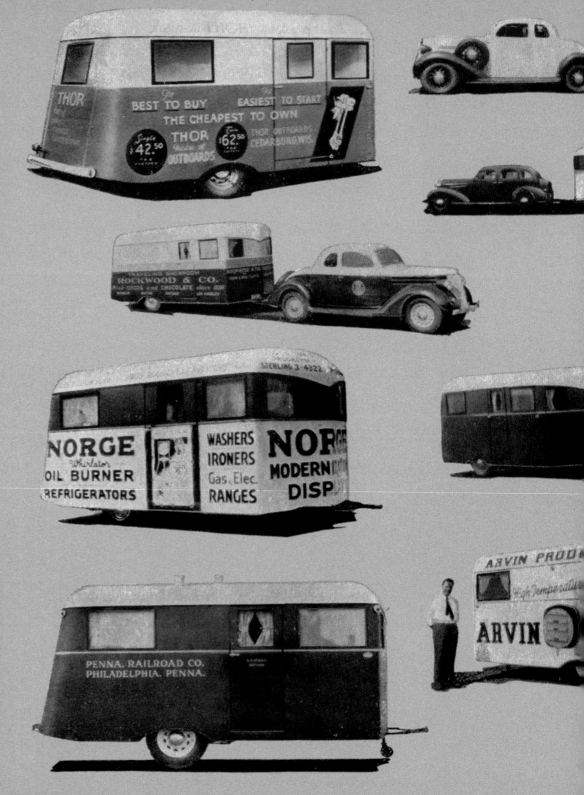

POPULAR

HOMECRAFT

The Home Workshop Magazine

SEPT OCT 1938

35¢

12 EXCLUSIVE PHOTOS
Tool Arrangement in the Philadelphia Home Workshop Guild

PORTABLE SOLARIUM

COLORED CONCRETE FLAGSTONES
MITRE BOX MARQUETRY
FOLDING UTILITY TABLE
PORTABLE SOLARIUM
WEATHER VANES
TOTEM POLES

build it yourself

TRAVELING SHOWCASE NO. 1

INLAND HOMES

AMERICA'S F...

TOWN HOUSES

APARTMENT HOU...

GROVER MYERS
Foot of Main Street Bridge — Little Rock, Ark.

ABC WASHERS and IRONERS

ABC *America's leading* WASHERS and IRONERS
Phone 4-3479

JANUARY, 1939

Automobile and Trailer Travel

MAGAZINE

★

In This Issue

Some Personal Items in a
Trailerite's Notebook ....
CORNELIUS VANDERBILT, JR.

An Answer to Unreasonable
Municipal Regulation ....
LAURENCE M. FINE

A.T.T.A. Officers Launch
Organization's Activities ....
KARL HALE DIXON

Trailerite Associations
Ready for Winter Meetings ....
AL J. SWEENEY

Trailerites Prepared for
New York's World's Fair.

Coach Manufacturers Find
Unity in Association Plans ....
WALTER O'REILLY

20¢

THE MAGAZINE OF MOTORIZED TRAVEL IN AMERICA

SERVICE SHOP   FACTORY SERVICE
BABSON BROS. CO. CHICAGO, ILL.

KINGFISHER
FISHING TACKLE
EDW. K. TRYON Co.
PHILADELPHIA

The trailer was an invaluable tool for the health-care community. People in rural areas didn't always have access to good doctors, and trailers could easily bring them to those areas. The model featured above and to the right was built in 1937 by the U.S. Public Health Service to fight syphilis.

THE HEALTH CLINIC COMES TO THE PEOPLE

THE AMERICAN CANCER SOCIETY
MOBILE INFORMATION CENTER

LOS ANGELES COUNTY BRANCH

THIS EXHIBIT IS A KEY TO KNOWLEDGE

PRESENTED BY THE
LOS ANGELES COUNTY BRANCH
OF THE
AMERICAN CANCER SOCIETY

MOBILE
FIRST AID STATION
DEMONSTRATION UNIT
MEDICAL DIVISION
In Cooperation With
Transportation Division
Courtesy of
TRAILER COACH
ASSOCIATION
LOS ANGELES
CIVILIAN DEFENSE
PAN AMERICAN & UNIVERSAL
TRAILER COACH CO.

MOBILE
FIRST AID STATION
DEMONSTRATION UNIT
MEDICAL DIVISION
In Cooperation With
Transportation Division
Courtesy of
TRAILER COACH
ASSOCIATION
LOS ANGELES
CIVILIAN DEFENSE

MOBILE OFFICE
YOUR CONGRESSMAN
Syd Herlong

HERE TO SERVE YOU

ROLLING *around* AMERICA

By
Robert R. Reynolds
*United States Senator
from North Carolina*

Senator Reynolds in Washington with his coupe and trailer at the start
of his tour of America, and map showing his route

TRAVEL, with its many broadening influences, should be a major course, required in every man's education.

Travel is expensive only if you choose to make it expensive. It can be as cheap as staying at home. Our roads are good, our automobiles are relatively cheap, the cost of fuel is low, and food and lodging, if you look for them in the right places, are not high.

I nursed a pet theory for a long time before I was able to try it out. I believed it was possible to spend thirty days seeing America from coast to coast, and from Canada to Mexico, at a total cost of $100 per person in actual travel expenses. And by seeing America I don't mean racing from dawn to dark along the highways until you're so tired driving you can't sleep and so sleepy you can't drive.

I mean visiting the beauty spots and the places rich in historical traditions, soaking in the atmosphere, letting the imagination fold back the pages of history, learning to know the places you have read about and viewing the great industrial centers and agricultural sections.

I took a thirty-day trip through America. I drove 11,500 miles—and did all the driving myself. I visited thirty-one states and the District of Columbia. I touched both coasts, drove through Ontario in Canada and took a glimpse of Juarez, Mex-

679

ROSALIE JONES DILL
FOR CONGRESS
MEETING HERE

Politics . . . you can't escape them, and the travel trailer was the perfect way for politicians to hit the road. Sadly, Rosalie Jones Dill did not win her bid for Congress.

Trailer Church Carries Services to Remote Areas

DIOCESAN MISSIONARY FATHERS
316 East Marshall Street
RICHMOND, VIRGINIA

SAINT MARY OF THE HIGHWAYS CHAPEL
CATHOLIC DIOCESE OF RICHMOND, VIRGINIA

"*Saint Mary of the Highways Chapel*" is a trailer chapel owned by the Catholic Diocese of Richmond, Virginia and operated in the 34,808 sq. mi. of the diocese by the Diocesan Missionary Fathers. Designed by Geo. F. Chaplin, it was built in 1938 and paid for by generous friends of the missions. It has an altar which can be used interiorly or exteriorly, a confessional, stations of the cross, and all church equipment besides living quarters and accommodations for two priests. A public address system, radio and victrola equipment as well as a motion picture projector help the missionaries bring to catholics and non-catholics, in rural areas, in military camps the Word of God. It was dedicated by Bishop Ireton at the Richmond Cathedral Feb. 26, 1939.

You are invited to visit the Chapel on the road, or at our home in Richmond.

Rev. Christopher Sullivan, O. M. C.
The First Trailer Chapel to go to China

JOIN THE FRANCISCAN MISSIONARY CRUSADE

Altar in the Trailer Chapel

Photographic Match Book - Produced by The Garraway Company, Rutherford, N. J., U. S. A.

Before the likes of Pat Robertson and *The 700 Club,* the clergy needed a way to tend to their far-flung flock. With a trailer, you could travel anywhere a car could go and take your pulpit with you. Live in the front and administer out the back . . . it was the perfect "mobile mission."

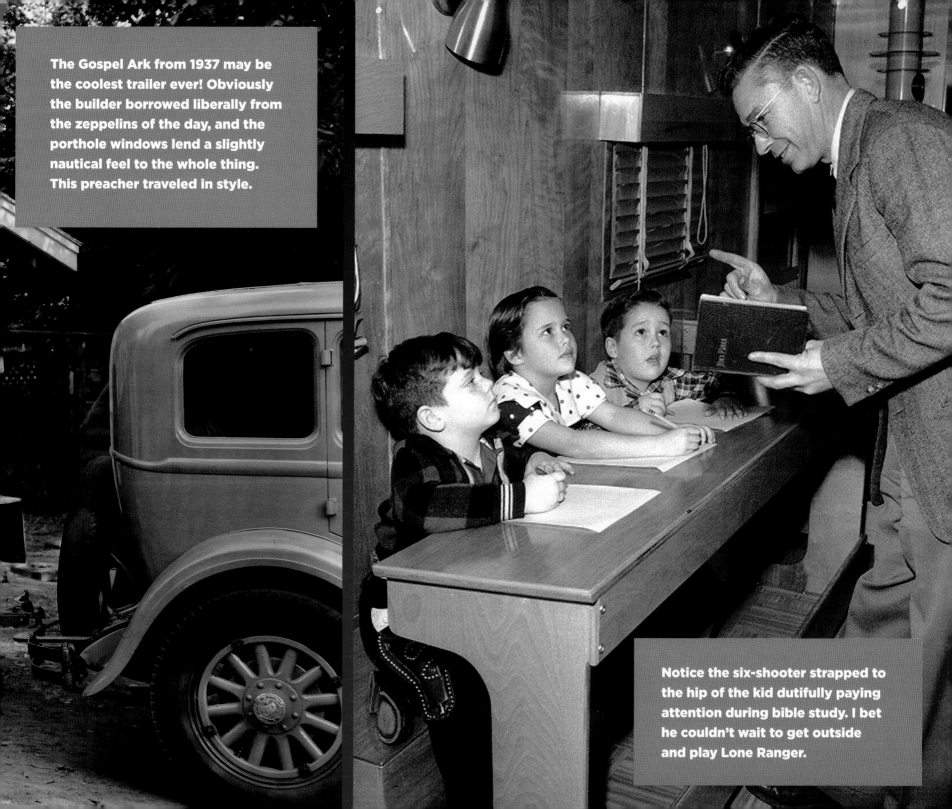

The Gospel Ark from 1937 may be the coolest trailer ever! Obviously the builder borrowed liberally from the zeppelins of the day, and the porthole windows lend a slightly nautical feel to the whole thing. This preacher traveled in style.

Notice the six-shooter strapped to the hip of the kid dutifully paying attention during bible study. I bet he couldn't wait to get outside and play Lone Ranger.

Trailer Parks

Going South

When trailer people are anxious
To leave the snow and ice,
A visit to the Red Coconut
At Fort Myers Beach would be nice.
Among the waving palms
And beneath the sunny skies
In an ideal trailer park
Like this, time flies.

White sands and balmy breezes
One forgets the Northern's freezes
Bathing beauties in the sun
Toasting themselves just for fun
Make the snow banks distant seem
As the Red Coconut Joy is Queen
Come you travelers, one and all
Join the Red Coconut's glad Roll Call.

—Advertisement for the Red Coconut Trailer
Park, Fort Myers Beach, Florida, 1949

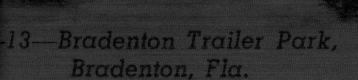

-13—Bradenton Trailer Park,
Bradenton, Fla.

LAKE DEER TRAILER PARK

WINTER HAVEN, FLA.

WINTER HAVEN – POLK COUNTY FLORIDA

TRAILER PARK

WHERE TO "UNHITCH"
Along the Coast.

SANTA BARBARA to SAN DIEGO

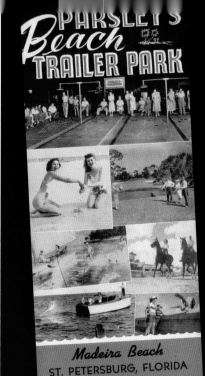

PARSLEY'S Beach TRAILER PARK

PARSLEY'S TRAILER PARK has its own wide private beach in front of the park, complete with beach umbrellas, chairs, outdoor fireplaces, and all the other paraphenalia of luxurious beach life. The beach is clean and safe—ideal for swimming and sun-bathing.

Center of attraction in the Park is the shuffleboard area and the Community Hall. The Hall is equipped with tables for card parties, coke machine, and library.

The many recreation facilities of St. Petersburg and the Beaches are available to our guests. Among the more popular of these are golf, tennis, flying, bowling, dog racing, theaters, horse racing, riding, etc.

Madeira Beach
ST. PETERSBURG, FLORIDA

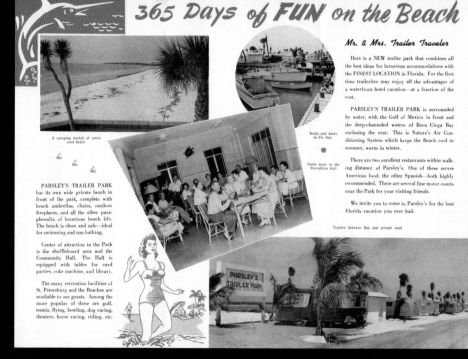

365 Days of FUN on the Beach

Mr. & Mrs. Trailer Traveler

Here is a NEW trailer park that combines all the best ideas for luxurious accommodations with the FINEST LOCATION in Florida. For the first time trailerites may enjoy all the advantages of a waterfront hotel vacation—at a fraction of the cost.

PARSLEY'S TRAILER PARK is surrounded by water, with the Gulf of Mexico in front and the deep-channeled waters of Boca Ciega Bay enclosing the rear. This is Nature's Air Conditioning System which keeps the Beach cool in summer, warm in winter.

There are two excellent restaurants within walking distance of Parsley's. One of these serves American food, the other Spanish—both highly recommended. There are several fine motor courts near the Park for your visiting friends.

We invite you to come to Parsley's for the best Florida vacation you ever had.

A sweeping stretch of white sand beach

Boats and docks on the Bay

Game room in the Recreation Hall

Trailers between Bay and private road

PARSLEY'S TRAILER PARK

ALASKA'S FINEST

WHITE BIRCH TRAILER PARK

Tile showers, Sanitary rest rooms,
Modern laundry, City water, Electric
Inspected by——Territorial Health De[pt.]

Box 1488 ANCHORAGE, ALASKA

The trailer park . . . much maligned and misunderstood, the home to millions of weary travelers and often the destination at the end of a thousand-mile trip. Florida and California have been attracting "snowbirds" since the advent of the car and decent roads. The travel trailer was the perfect way to enjoy all the comforts of home in a beautiful and warm spot. Whether you liked golf, fishing, square dancing or just lounging, the trailer park was your home away from home. As we trailerites like to say, "Home is where you park it."

for gracious living . . . .

VALLEY TRAILER PARK

California's

MODEL TRAILER PARK

LOOK FOR THE UNIQUE "TRAILER" SIGN
—SHAPED EXACTLY LIKE ONE OF
CALIFORNIA'S FINE TRAILER COACHES

VALLEY Trailer PARK

Prize-winner of the 1948 Beautification Contest

A beautiful view
The ideal central location of VALLEY PARK affords a splendid view of the mountainous horizon.

Shaded areas
Eucalyptus and other native California trees further enhance the grounds.

The prize-winning garden in VALLEY PARK was a blaze of colorful bloom, with Fuchsias, Pelargoniums, snapdragons, pansies, Schizanthus, and many other beautiful varieties. It was judged on the qualities of neatness, color harmony, general design, and selection and condition of plant material. There were prizes galore! Not only did the management present numerous awards, but a great many local merchants generously participated. Everyone at VALLEY PARK received prizes for their efforts in this contest.

This contest and many other activities of VALLEY PARK have been given local and national recognition.

Large areas
Each area, averaging 1054 sq. ft., insures maximum privacy and provides ample space for trailer, car, flower beds, and a spacious lawn. There's a cement patio for each trailer.

Paved streets and walks
The entire park is permeated with 20 ft. paved streets, and a 6 ft. walk divides the park into two sections.

BREAK AND SWING!

111

California
"Here I Come"

Hollywood Park

TRAILER LODGE - INGLEWOOD, CALIFORNIA

There were more travel trailer companies in California than any other state in the union, and for good reason. Great weather, close proximity to the beach, desert and mountains, plus plenty of good jobs in the aircraft industry, made California the place to be after WWII, and the state's trailer parks were some of the best in the country.

RECREATION MOBILE HOMES PARK — MONTEREY, CALIFORNIA

WESTLAND TRAILER CITY

**6665 LONG BEACH BOULEVARD
LONG BEACH, CALIFORNIA
R. E. Robson, Owner**

Modern, 10 Acres
Paved Streets, Grass Lots, Shade
Clean Rest Rooms, Plenty Hot Water
Convenient Bus Service
20 Minutes to Downtown Los Angeles
10 Minutes to the Beach
No Dogs, Adults Only

"CALIFORNIA'S FINEST"

3B-H1563

WILLOW TRAILER PARK, LONG BEACH, CALIFORNIA

GREENWOOD TRAILER COURT, SAN DIEGO, CALIFORNIA

Florida
"Wish You Were Here"

P. G. 17   MUNICIPAL TOURIST CAMP AND COMMUNITY HALL ON CHARLOTTE HARBOR, PUNTA GORDA, FLA.

6A-H1196

136 ONE OF THE MANY TRAILER CAMPS IN THE SUNSHINE STATE, FLORIDA

A Modern Trailer Park   Florida

0B-H1524

76—Aerial View of Municipal Trailer Park, Tampa, Fla.

Where else in the United States can you go in the dead of winter and enjoy warm weather, sandy beaches and plenty of palm trees swaying in the breeze? Florida has always held the crown for home of the world's best trailer parks, and millions of trailerites flock there to this day to enjoy the spectacular climate and friendly Floridians.

Bradenton Trailer Park, Bradenton, Florida—40

World's Largest Trailer Park, Bradenton, Florida

950 A Florida Modern Trailer Park

G136 ONE OF THE MANY TRAILER CAMPS IN THE SUNSHINE STATE, FLORIDA

These beautiful watercolors painted by artist Joseph Golinkin appeared in a 1937 issue of *Fortune* magazine in an article titled "200,000 Trailers."

In post-war America, five dollars a day was a pretty penny, but that's what it would have cost you to park your bouncing bungalow at Ollie Trout's Trailer Park. Ollie guaranteed palm trees on every site, and there was a bevy of white-jacketed servants delivering cold drinks and warm food to your trailer door.

Ollie Trout's
"America's Finest Trailer Park"

OLLIE TROUT'S PARK, TRAILER PARADISE, BISCAYNE BLVD. AT 107TH ST., MIAMI, FLORIDA

AMERICA'S FINEST TRAILER PARK

Ollie Trouts Tourist Park
107th St., Biscayne Blvd.
Miami, Fla.

OLLIE TROUT'S PARK
Trailer Paradise, 10600 Biscayne Blv., Miami, Fla.

America's Finest Trailer Park

1919 1998

TOURISTS

PIONEER AUTOMOBILE CAMPERS ORGANIZATION

The Tin Can Tourists were organized at Desoto Park in Tampa, Florida, in 1919. The group, known for the soldered tin cans on their radiator caps, had the objective "to unite fraternally all autocampers." The initiation process for prospective members included a secret handshake, sign and password. After singing the official song, "The More We Get Together," the trailerite was an official member of the Tin Can Tourists of the World. Membership had fallen off by 1968, and by the mid-1980s the club was no longer in existence, but in 1998 Forrest and Jeri Bone lovingly renewed the club. Now with their son Terry at the helm the Tin Can Tourists are the club of choice for the vintage trailer set.

Tin Can Tourists Convene

DON'T laugh. It is a real live organization composed of touring fans—who tour in—well you know the kind of car they make jokes about. And once a year as many members of the organization as can make the riffle drive the old "Tin Can" to some part of the world and there meet in road convention with several thousand other members. Tourists from Portland, Oregon, and Portland, Me., meet and swap tales of travel.

This picture was recently taken at Gainsville, Fla., where a group of the tourists held a jubilee and parade. The next convention is to be held in Florida in the month of December. At least 5,000 cars are expected to be present. At the annual convention officers for the ensuing year are elected. The highest office in the organization is that of Royal Tin Can Opener. There are many women members of the association.

The picture shows Glen A. Whipple, editor of the official organ, the "Tin Can Tourist," in front of the camp grounds.

324.   A "TIN CAN TOURIST CAMP" IN FLORIDA.

"A TIN CAN TOURIST" CAMP IN FLORIDA.

'Neath spreading oak and pine tree tall
"A tin can tourist" in the Fall
Puts up his tent and plans to stay
In Florida till blooming May,
And soon another tourist comes,
They meet and greet like old time chums,
They tell new jokes and make new plans,
And mess from out the same tin cans.

Then other tourists come along,
The camp force now is growing strong
Cars from the North, the East, the West,
Bring weary tourists seeking rest,
All happy in this flowery glade
Beneath the broad oaks welcome shade
They're singing songs and making plans
And piling up the empty cans.

And ere the blooming May comes round
They'll buy a piece of fertile ground
And mark it off in streets and squares
And every tourist take some shares,
For they will build a city here
When they come back another year
Just as the "tin can tourist" plans
When he piles up the empty cans.

—Ruth Raymond

VERSE COPYRIGHTED BY ASHEVILLE POST CARD CO.

105348

What a full day! Between watering the lawn, fixing the kids' bike and cooking dinner, it's a wonder there's time for anything else. But our model squeezes in some reading, TV time and a nice bedtime smoke. Life is good in the trailer park.

The postcard is as American as apple pie, and the trailer postcard has a special place on the pie rack. Often risqué and always over-the-top, the trailer and the trailer park were favorite subjects for the artists who pumped out these miniature works of art. There's a lot of potty humor, men behaving badly and a little dog barking furiously. These little gems are just plain fun!

Not A Care In The World

6B-H860

I liked to read stories of wandering knights
And their exploits as told in the books,
But I do my wanderings comfortably
In a trailer that's ultra de luxe.

© C. T. & CO.

"On Our Way—Enjoying the Comforts of Home—
Try Out This Idea Some Time!"

W218

HURRY UP
TH' MILKING,
DAUGHTER!

FRESH MILK

FRESH EGGS

COPYRIGHT BY
E. C. KROPP CO.
MILWAUKEE, WIS.

HOME, SWEET HOME ON THE TRAIL

C-142

6A-H1996

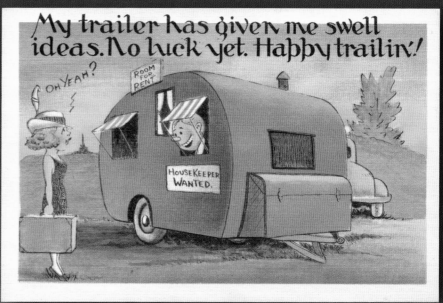

To say Bill O'Malley was a prolific cartoonist is an understatement. Not only did he fill the pages of various trailer magazines, he was also a frequent contributor to *The Saturday Evening Post, Life* and *Sports Illustrated.* His cartoons ran from the thirties into the seventies. I love the exhausted stork chasing the trailer with the expectant mother in the back.

Kodachrome
SLIDE

Kodak PROCESSED BY KODAK

Being an avid fly-fisherman, I am drawn to images that depict anglers. Trailerites love to fish, and often in fabulous outfits. I wish I looked that good while I was out thrashing the water in search of trout.

·HUNTING·FISHING· SPORTS·
Edited by DICK WOOD

What's better then grabbing your honey, packing up the trailer and heading out on a romantic holiday in the land yacht? There is nothing nicer then snuggling up in the cozy bunk of a trailer parked next to the ocean on a sunny day. And the great thing is that you can drive on and wake up the next day in the mountains and you don't even have to unpac your suitcase.

So!!
You're Going
To
Retire

VACATIONERS

1951 Paul & me when we lived in trailer

I've always imagined this young couple was on their honeymoon at the start of a long life together. It's a very unusual trailer; the door is on the back, as opposed to the side, which may mean it's homemade.

I'm pretty sure that's a baby bump under her frock, and hopefully her soldier stayed out of whatever war we were fighting at that time so they could enjoy their new home-on-wheels when junior showed up.

The lovely ladies and their trailers. Whether getting married, getting ready for work or just plain hanging around, the gals always make the campsite a whole lot sunnier.

Outside their trailer at Yosemite National Park, the Halleson sisters practice their act for the nightly programs at Camp Curry, Yosemite Lodge and the Ahwahnee Hotel. In winter the family goes by trailer to Death Valley to perform at Furnace Creek Inn. From left to right . . . Diane, 7, who sings; Letty Mae, accordionist; Nancy, 12, singer; Beatrice, 17, at the bass viol.

The gents! In our coats and ties or snazzy uniforms, or dressed up like a sheik from an Errol Flynn movie, we are always ready for adventure, or at least a good lounge chair and a cold beer.

$15 PER MONTH
CHILDREN WELCOME

Trailer kids are as cute as they come, and these three get a little help from the Wonder Bread box they are perched on.

You can't beat a big wedge of watermelon on a hot summer day! These four are happy campers.

July 1970

Dad's Trailer Baltoa

1573

Phyis + Harvey   1944-45

Do you think the dad
took this snap is mo
of that gun or his ba

There is nothing like your first bike, and these munchkins are happy to pose with their new set of wheels.

Yes, that is a raccoon on his shoulder; and yes, that is a squirrel on his head; and yes, that is a dog on the roof of his car . . . and don't forget the Chihuahua in the window. Trailerites love their pets!

FEB · 55

OCT · 57 ·

Since the invention of the automobile, families have been figuring out ways to make travel more comfortable by bringing along as many of the creature comforts from home as they could fit on the jalopy. The travel trailer was the perfect solution, so Mom, Dad and the kids have been rolling along for close to a hundred years and the RV craze is not slowing down.

You gotta love the tiny Christmas tree crammed into the parlor of the trailer. People love to celebrate the holidays, and trailerites will take any excuse to decorate their happy little homes. If you think your house smells piney after you put up the tree, just imagine a one-hundred-square-foot trailer!

CUSTOMLINE

THE TRULY MODERN SANTA CLAUS TRAVELS BY TRAILER

LIBERTY COACH COMPANY, INC.

BREMEN, INDIANA

TRAILER DEALER

The Trade Magazine for the Trailercoach Industry

For you nontrailerites, that's the trailer's "chimney" Santa is pondering.

DECEMBER 1956

TRAILER Topics MAGAZINE

20¢ PER COPY
$2.00 PER YEAR

THE LARGEST AND MOST INFLUENTIAL MOBILEHOME MAGAZINE

WESTERN *Trailer Life*

DECEMBER, 1947
TEN CENTS

Merry Christmas

Toys, Knickknacks

and Other
COLLECTIBLES

Trailers worked their way into all aspects of popular culture, and the toy and game market was no exception. All those little trailerites needed something to play with.

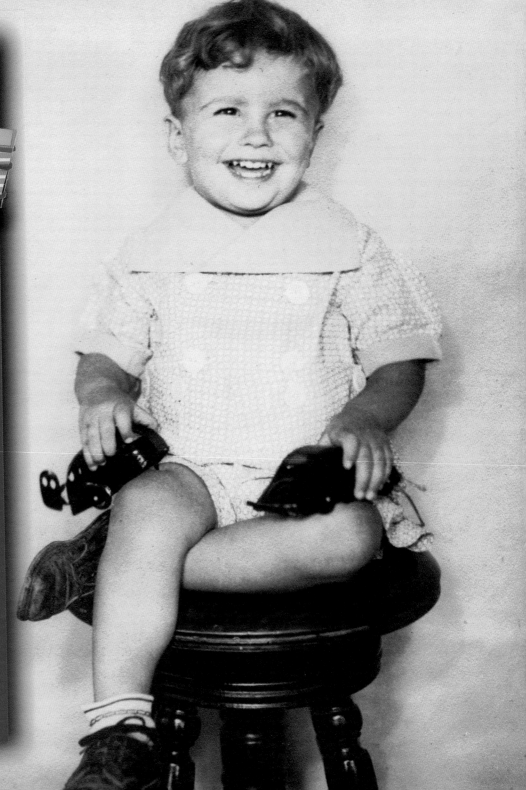

PAPER DOLL FAMILY
AND THEIR *Trailer*

Florence Salter

COPYRIGHT 1939
MERRILL PUBLISHING CO.
CHICAGO, ILLINOIS

3436
Printed in U.S.A.

CLOTHES for the FAMILY

LIVING ROOM

For you to make. Read ALL directions carefully before you start. Cut off this panel on dotted line. Cut out the objects. Match and paste each one on white space in the picture which has the same letter. Be careful NOT to cut on the other side. There are pictures on the other side.

Paper dolls were all the craze in the thirties, and these two examples feature the whole family, including Fido, of course.

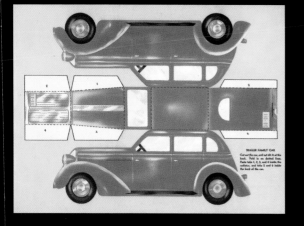

TRAILER FAMILY CAR

Cut out the car, and cut slit A at the back. Fold in on dotted lines. Paste tabs 1, 2, 3, and 4 inside the radiator, and tabs 5 and 6 inside the back of the car.

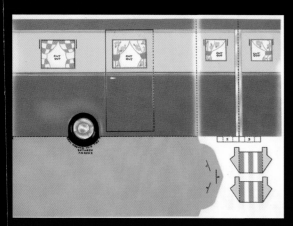

THE TRAILER FAMILY
CUTOUTS

DESIGNED by DOTTY DOWNS

Dorothy Downs

No. 2169

COPYRIGHT MCMXXXVII
THE SAALFIELD PUBLISHING COMPANY
AKRON, OHIO
MADE IN U. S. A.
REGISTERED AT STATIONERS' HALL.

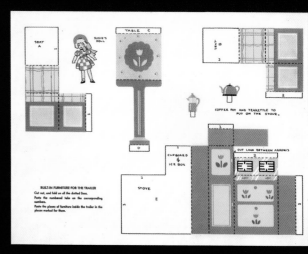

SEAT A   SUSIE'S DOLL   TABLE C   SEAT B

COFFEE POT AND TEAKETTLE TO PUT ON THE STOVE.

CUPBOARD & ICE BOX   CUT LINE BETWEEN ARROWS

STOVE

BUILT-IN FURNITURE FOR THE TRAILER

Cut out, and fold on all the dotted lines.
Paste the numbered tabs on the corresponding numbers.
Paste the pieces of furniture inside the trailer in the places marked for them.

This game from 1937 has some great graphics, and with a villain named "Terry the Terrible Speed Cop," it's a hoot to play. Funny thing is, the whole point of the game is to be Terry, and the winner has the "privilege" of keeping his badge for the next game.

The JOLLY JUMP-UPS
TRADE MARK REG. U.S. PAT. OFF.
VACATION TRIP
Copyright MCMXLII by
McLOUGHLIN BROS., INC.
Springfield, Mass.
2922 Made in U.S.A.
by Geraldyne Clyne

Bridge tally cards.

Commemorative plates.

Salt and pepper shakers.

Matchbook dispenser with joke matchbooks.

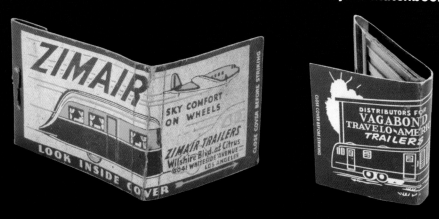

Advertising matchbooks.

Valentines and greeting cards were a great way to stay in touch with that special trailerite in your life.

This 1936 windup Marx coupe and Lonesome Pine trailer were sold as a set, and are the epitome of thirties cool. They look like something out of a Tex Avery cartoon and I keep expecting a wolf dressed in a zoot suit to step out of the car.

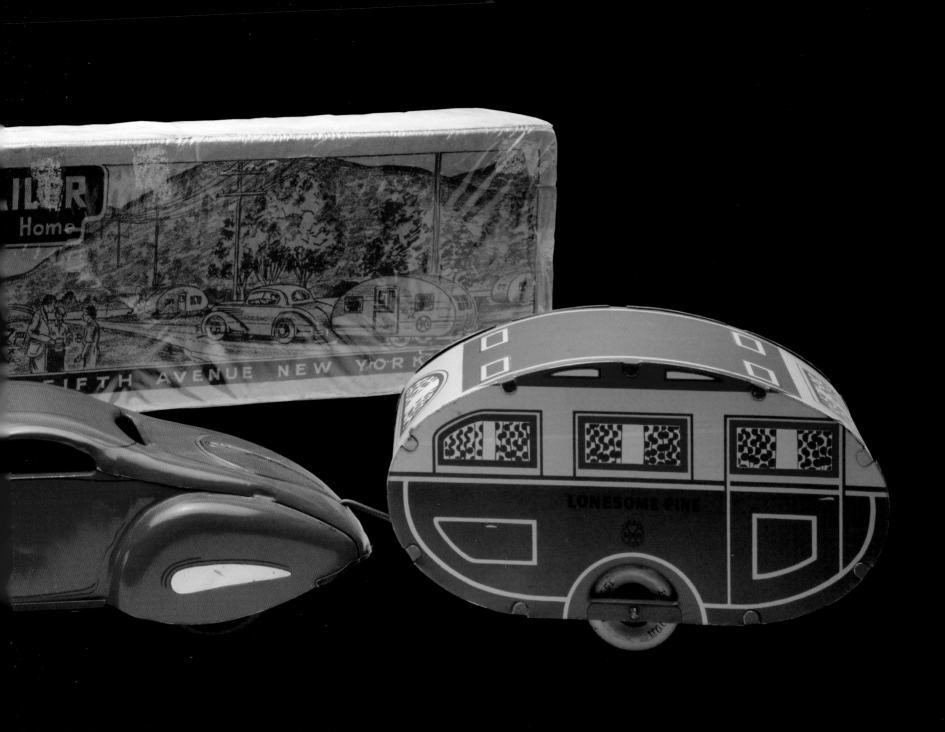

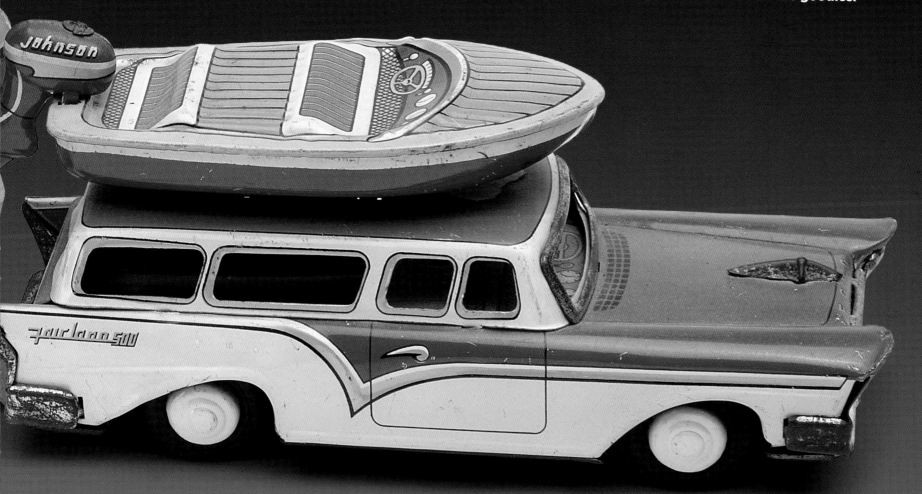

Made in Japan in 1955, this set has all the goodies.

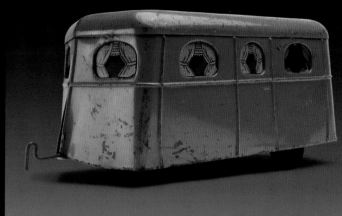

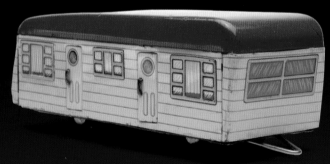

657

CAMPING TRAILER
WITH FORD STATION WAGON

Conclusion

THINK of yourself as owning a home with a thousand addresses . . . of being near your job and your favorite recreation . . . of stepping out the front door and viewing the grandeur of America . . . of securing the benefits of travel, the fun of new freedom of living and good wholesome, healthful outdoor life. Think of the low cost of the Trailer Coach, its comfort and convenience, its complete furnishings and equipment. Think, too, of dozens of other uses you can get from Trailer Coach ownership, including use in your own job or business. Then you'll agree that . . .

The Trailer Coach OFFERS MORE IN THE AMERICAN WAY OF LIFE THAN ANY OTHER PRODUCT . . .

Couldn't have said it better myself. This wrap-up from a 1947 brochure extolling the virtues of the travel trailer is the perfect end to our road trip together, and remember: Home is where you haul it!